The Ultimate
VENISON
COOKBOOK for
DEER CAMP

The Ultimate VENISON COOKBOOK for DEER CAMP

Harold Webster, Jr.

GREAT AMERICAN PUBLISHERS

WWW.GREATAMERICANPUBLISHERS.COM

TOLL-FREE 1.888.854.5954

Great American Publishers

501 Avalon Way, Suite B • Brandon, MS 39047

TOLL-FREE 1.888.854.5954

www.GreatAmericanPublishers.com

ISBN 978-1-934817-31-5

10 9 8 7 6 5 4 3 2 1
First edition

This book is dedicated to my parents; Harold W. Webster, Sr. and Ann L. Webster.

It was Dad who taught me how to hunt and fish and it was with him that I spent my first night at deer camp.

It was Mom who taught me the basics of cooking and it was with her that I spent my formative years standing on her kitchen stool and learning.

However, it was from both of them that I learned

how to prepare wild game, fowl and fish and to appreciate nature's bounty that surrounded me.

Neither Mom nor Dad ever had the opportunity to read any of my published words, but it was their unconditional love that molded and shaped every single letter.

ACKNOWLEDGMENTS

Jim and Darlene Wilson - Ozark Mountain Outfitters, Houston, MO

Bob Mizek - New Archery Products, Forest Park, IL

Eric Wilson - Ozark Mountain Outfitters, Houston, MO

Randy Wood - TenPoint Crossbow Technologies, Suffield, OH

Rob Dykeman - Excalibur Crossbows, Kitchener, Ontario, Canada

Butch Hedrickson - Butch & Wendy's Hunting Adventures,
    Center Point, TX

Danny Miller - Horizontal Archery, Sardis, OH

Ron Khosla - CoolBot, Huguenot Street Farm in New Paltz, NY

Dorge O. Huang - Firenock, Henry, IL

Wendy White - Butch & Wendy's Hunting Adventures,
    Center Point, TX

Dan Hendricks - Horizontal Bowhunter Magazine, Glenwood, MN

Lee Zimmerman - Tallmadge, OH

Bill Roundaville - Leakesville, MS

Mike Campbell - Grenada, MS

Robin Dambrino - Grenada, MS

Joe Tubbs - Jackson, MS

Ottie Snyder - New Matamoras, OH

Curtis Breland - Leakesville, MS

John Collins - Tupelo, MS

Randy Hayman - Raymond, MS

Charles and Jane Ivy - Raymond, MS

Contents

Introduction

Spending time at a deer camp is a memorable outdoors experience and the food we eat should be memorable also.

This book was written for those Bubba's and Bubbaleen's, who like me, enjoy spending a portion of our outdoor time at a deer camp and who also enjoy eating our harvest amongst friends.

Cooking at deer camp does not have to be difficult or complicated and there is no reason not to enjoy good food and have fun in the outdoors at the same time. Some of the best and also some of the most unappetizing venison that I have ever eaten were both served at deer camps. These less than appetizing meals are probably the reason that I decided to research and to teach myself how to selectively harvest and to prepare venison for the table in the first place.

The best venison I have eaten was at a small hunting club. It was this meal that gave me the inspiration for Oven-Baked Venison Loin with Blackberry Sauce. The most unappetizing venison I have eaten—I won't tell where this camp is located because they are great people, good friends and they have been very nice to me. Anne was with me the night we were invited to stay at that camp for a late meal of "Slice-It-Thin" and "Fry-It-Hard" venison round steak. As we were driving away, Anne sat there staring out the front window of the car and said, "That was not quite as good as the venison we eat at home." Miss Anne is a true southern girl and is the master of the tactful understatement.

I am of the opinion that the real source of the unappetizing meals I have eaten at hunting camps is the absence of specific deer camp cooking literature. It has been my observation that most men folk who cook at deer camp do not cook at home and require detailed instructions—I know this to be true because I am one of those folks.

I have spent many long hours sitting in my tree stand thinking long and hard about the things I enjoy the most and the things I enjoy the least about eating at deer camps. I finally came to the realization that my primary dislike was the boring redundancy of eating the same one or two things over and over again. Venison sausage for breakfast is nice and fried venison loin steaks, with white rice and brown gravy, make a fine dinner— but not for every breakfast and not for every dinner.

I decided that if what I wanted was variation, then I would have to expand my thinking about how I approached my personal deer camp cooking and apply some of the techniques I learned from my mother. When I was a young boy, my ol' granddad once told me, "Harold, Jr., everything in life is a tradeoff. What are you willing to trade?" Trade? But, at what cost and what would I be giving up? My thoughts, regarding variation, went in several different directions at the same time and sometimes these directions were in conflict:

- A selection of relatively simple recipes
- Minimal time in the kitchen
- Minimal pot washing
- Breaking the monotony of eating the same things
- Minimal items in the pantry
- The cost and availability of ingredients in rural grocery stores
- Lack of 'enthusiastic' help in the kitchen
- Special meals for celebrations and the occasional honored visitor

To meet these eight conditions, the minimalist pantry would have to be expanded—just a little, but most of these additions to the pantry would also have to be readily available in most small town/rural grocery stores.

I think I have been successful in developing and adapting a variety of recipes that will break the monotony, while at the same time maintaining the spirit of fellowship I have come to associate with life in a deer camp. I also think I have been successful in keeping the items in the pantry at a minimum or at least easily obtainable and at an affordable cost. And, the recipes are within easy reach for those Bubbas and Bubbaleens among us who may not normally spend a great deal of time in the kitchen.

Finding someone or several members to do the cooking reminds me of a story that my ol' granddad once told me. The rule in his circa 1920 deer camp was if you ever complained about the food, you had to cook until the next person complained. It seems this particular year no one would complain about the food and the first "volunteer" cook could not get any relief from the kitchen.

This bunch of guys loved venison chili, so the "volunteer" cook told the guys they were going to have chili for dinner the next night. To make sure someone complained and complained loudly, when the next night rolled around, he emptied a whole box of salt into the chili and he then sat back and waited for the first complaint. The older members knew about the complaining trick, so some of them silently got up from the table and emptied their bowls back into the pot. One of the newer members almost forgot about the rule and blurted out, "This chili sure is SALTY," and then remembering the rule, quickly added, "But, ain't it good."

Good deer camp cooks are sometimes hard to find and convincing folks that cooking is relatively easy and enjoyable can be even more difficult. Cooking at deer camp is not hard, it does not require long hours in the kitchen, it does not require a professional cook (although nice), it does not require exotic ingredients and it does not require years of cooking experience. But what it does require is a bit of imagination, a desire to enjoy good food with friends, a little thought and above all it requires:

- Selectively harvesting game that is suitable for the table.
- Game that has been properly cared for from the field to the table.
- A simple menu, but at the same time, with a measured level of creativity and variation.
- Enjoyment in the company of good friends.

It was my intent in writing this book to assist others like me to approach their deer camp cooking as a time to enjoy the fruits of our harvests. Many of us may have many trophies hanging on the wall, but we can also enjoy taking our hunting experience to its ultimate conclusion—enjoying the bounty of our harvest amongst friends.

BROIL, GRILL or SKILLET-FRY?

I grew up believing that you could not successfully broil, grill or skillet-fry venison round steaks—or any venison steak for that matter. Anyway, that was what I was told. I tried it a few times and I was not successful; so I stayed with moist cooking. I had also never wondered if there were any T-bone steaks in a deer. Not only are there T-bone steaks, but when cut thick, they are delicious.

Cut steak about 1 to 1¼ inches thick and quickly cook to no more than 138° to 140° internal temperature and remove from heat.

When considering whether to broil, grill or skillet-fry venison round, T-bone or loin steaks, there are several things you should consider:

- Just like beef in the meat market, there is a natural tenderness in the different cuts of meat.
- Where are these cuts located on the animal?
- How would you cook a similar cut of meat if it came from a cow?

About 1972, I was invited to hunt at a small camp. I knew the area well. For the previous five years, this had been one of the areas that I drove through every few weeks. After tiring of driving the same roads, I began exploring and traveling the secondary roads. I don't know if you have ever heard of the old Swinging Bridge that is located just northwest of Mountain View, Arkansas, but I remember when it was open to automobile traffic. The camp was located in a valley some ten miles east of the Swinging Bridge. This camp was an Ozark Mountain classic that had once been the home of substance mountain farmers.

An Old Kitchen

The main room sported a native stone fireplace on the left wall with a well-worn and elbow-polished table and several oak benches in the center of the room. There was an old double rope-sprung bed pushed up against the back wall and several low-sitting single beds in the small loft above. Around the walls, you could still see the pegs stuck into the boards that once served to hang cloths, pots, chairs, and the other items of necessity that a mountain family might have had on hand. The floors were dusty and well polished by years of bare feet.

Underneath the dusty table was a remnant of a rag rug; the main room was bare and unpretentious. At the rear was a small kitchen with a small wood burning cook stove that had a small baking oven with a door that opened on the right side.

The Sylamore District of the Ozark National Forest is located in this area of the state and I was in the area to provide safety training for the U.S. Forest Service personnel working in the newly developed Blanchard Springs Cavern complex. My contact was a local gentleman who had been working for the U.S. Forest Service since he had graduated from the county high school. He was as fine a gentleman as anyone would ever wish to meet. At that time, there was no motel in Mountain View, so instead he invited me to overnight in his home.

It was my impression that folks had been using this old cabin as their hunting base since the 1950's and they were familiar with every slew, draw, rock, and spring within walking distance. Two of us had harvested nice young bucks that day and we were sitting around outside discussing what we were going to have for dinner. My friend asked one

of the guys if he would do some of his fancy butchering on our deer and I offered to lend a hand.

The man (I don't remember his name) was a professional butcher by trade. He went to his Jeep, brought out his knives and meat saw and we sawed through the backbone, just behind the last rib. Then he sawed off the next section to the rear (containing the tenderloin and a rear portion of loin). We carried that large section of meat and bone over to a large stump that served triple duty as a chair, something to chop kindling on, and a butcher block. He placed the meat on top and asked me to hold it tight on both sides so that he could saw it down the middle. He then sawed each side into approximately 1½-inch-thick pieces of steak. And then I saw it. What I was holding in my hand were small T-bone steaks. These T-bone steaks were not as large as those from a cow, but they were larger than pork chops. We cut six nice steaks from each side.

The butcher and I gathered up the steaks and we all went inside. It is always a little cool in late November in the mountains and, on most days, they kept a fire going in the fireplace. We pushed the logs aside and a large ¼-inch-thick piece of blackened steel boiler plate was placed on the andirons. The butcher asked me if I had ever eaten deer T-bone steaks and I said, "Not that I can recall."

He spread a small lump of lard over the steel plate and as soon as it began to smoke, he dropped on the T-bone steaks. They began to sizzle and in a minute or so you could smell the aroma of cooked meat. He flipped the steaks and as the second side was browning, he spread a spoonful of butter on top and waited for it to melt. When the second side had just browned, he removed the steaks and we all sat down at the table for dinner. It took a few minutes to slice the bread and pour the coffee before we could eat.

The butcher asked me, "So, how did you like them?"

What could I say, other than, "That was some mighty fine eating." I asked him, "What is the trick to making them so tender and juicy?"

He said, "You saw what I did. I cut them thick, I did not overcook them and we waited a few minutes before serving them."

STEAK

How to Cut Steaks

T-Bone Steaks:

T-bone steaks are made from the saddle, which is located between the last rib and the hindquarters. You can do it two ways:

1. Saw long ways down the saddle and then saw steaks off each side; or
2. Saw across the saddle and then saw down the middle of each piece to make two T-bone steaks. Cutting is easier if the saddle is chilled or slightly frozen before cutting.

- Saddle—which contains the loins and tenderloins
- Remove silver skin and white tissues from all sides of saddle
- First, saw down the length of the saddle. Then, saw (1¼ to 1½ inch) T-bone steaks from each side

Round Steak:

By their very nature, round steaks, whether they come from a cow or a deer, are a tougher cut of meat than a T-bone steak. Round steak comes from the hindquarter and T-bone steak comes from the section behind the ribs that contain both the loin and the tenderloin.

The best venison round steaks are cut from the large end of the hindquarter. If you do not have an electric meat saw, place the hindquarter in the refrigerator overnight and allow the meat to firm. Use a knife to cut around the hindquarter and then saw through the bone.

Venison round steaks can be used in any recipe in which you would use beef round steak. To broil or grill venison round steaks, they should be cut 1 inch (or more) thick and cooked to no more that 138° to 140°.

Simmered T-Bone Steak
with Lemon-Mushroom Sauce

3 tablespoons lemon juice

4 venison T-bone steaks,
    cut 1 inch thick

Salt and pepper to taste

1 teaspoon bacon drippings

2 tablespoons minced green
    onions

¼ pound mushrooms, sliced
    thin

½ clove garlic, minced fine

½ cup plus 1 teaspoon red wine,
    divided

1 teaspoon meat extract

½ bay leaf

1 teaspoon all-purpose flour

1 teaspoon butter, melted

Chopped fresh parsley

1 Pour lemon juice over the steaks and let marinate 10 minutes. Drain. Sprinkle with salt and pepper.

2 Heat bacon drippings in a heavy skillet over high heat. Add steaks. Brown 4 minutes on each side. Remove steaks and set aside.

3 Sauté green onions in pan drippings until lightly browned. Add mushrooms and garlic and sauté for a few minutes more. Add ½ cup red wine, meat extract and bay leaf; bring to a boil and simmer 5 minutes.

4 Put steaks in gravy and heat 3 minutes and then place them on a preheated platter. Keep warm.

5 Whisk together flour, butter and remaining 1 teaspoon red wine. Thicken gravy with flour mixture.

6 Pour some of gravy over steaks. Sprinkle with parsley. Serve remaining gravy on side.

SERVES 4

T-Bone Steak Flambé
in Cream Sauce

6 tablespoons butter

**4 venison T-bone steaks,
cut ½ to ¾ inch thick**

**6 tablespoons bourbon or dark
rum**

½ cup heavy cream

½ cup canned chicken broth

Salt and pepper to taste

Parsley sprigs

1 Melt butter in a skillet and brown steaks over high heat, about 3 minutes on each side. Do not overcook.

2 Pour butter off pan. Lower flame, remove skillet from burner. Pour bourbon down inside of edge of skillet, return skillet to stove and tip to ignite. Shake pan until flame dies. Remove steaks from pan to a warm platter and cover with aluminum foil to keep warm.

3 To skillet, add cream, chicken broth, salt and pepper; stir until thickened. Pour sauce over steaks, garnish with parsley sprigs.

SERVES 4

Steam-Baked T-Bone Steaks
with Rice and Tomatoes

INGREDIENTS

1 cup Sauterne wine

2 cups water

Juice of 1 lemon

6 venison T-bone steaks,
  cut 1 inch or more thick

Canola oil

Salt and pepper to taste

1 green bell pepper

2 cups cooked rice

1 medium onion, sliced

1 large tomato, sliced

2 (14-ounce) cans whole
  tomatoes

2 drops bitters

1 garlic clove, minced

1 For marinade, combine wine, water and lemon juice.

2 Place steaks in a large zip-close plastic bag and add marinade. Press out air from bag and seal. Refrigerate 6 to 8 hours.

3 Drain steaks and brown on both sides in hot oil. Season with salt and pepper. Place steaks in bottom of a large ovenproof baking dish.

4 Cut bell pepper into ¼-inch-thick rings. Place a ring on top of each steak. Put a scoop of rice into center of each pepper ring. Top rice with a slice of onion and top each onion slice with a slice of tomato.

5 Chop canned whole tomatoes into small chunks; add bitters and garlic and season with salt and pepper. Pour tomato mixture over and around steaks. Cover and steam 1 hour in 375° oven.

SERVES 6

Grilled T-Bone Steaks
with Bourbon Marinade

BOURBON MARINADE:

4 cups bourbon

¼ cup salad oil

2 tablespoons teriyaki or soy sauce

1 teaspoon Worcestershire sauce

2 cloves garlic, chopped fine

¼ teaspoon pepper

STEAKS:

4 venison T-bone steaks, cut 1½ to 2 inches thick

2 tablespoons butter

¼ cup chopped onion

¼ cup chopped green bell pepper

½ cup chopped celery

1 (8-ounce) can diced tomatoes

½ teaspoon sugar

⅛ teaspoon garlic powder

Salt and pepper to taste

Dijon mustard

1 To make **Bourbon Marinade**, combine all ingredients in 1-gallon zip-close plastic bag, mix well and add venison steaks. Refrigerate and marinate venison steaks 4 to 6 hours.

2 To cook **Steaks**, remove steaks from marinade and set aside to drain.

3 In saucepan, melt butter. Add onion, green bell pepper and celery. Cook until the onion turns just clear and set aside.

4 Add the tomatoes and their juice to vegetables. Cook over low heat 5 minutes. Add sugar and garlic powder. Season with salt and pepper and simmer 10 minutes.

5 Brush the venison steaks lightly with Dijon mustard and season with salt and pepper. Grill 5 minutes more or less per side. Do not overcook. Steaks should be cooked to rare or no more than medium rare (138° to 140°).

6 Spoon onion-tomato sauce on the center of each serving plate and lay on a venison steak.

SERVES 4

Blackened Venison Steak

What is blackening? Spices are rubbed into the surface of the meat, then the meat is quickly seared on an extremely hot and greaseless cast-iron surface until lightly charred on both sides. You may wish to cook this outside on a gas burner or on your barbecue grill. Be prepared: You will generate a large volume of smoke. The idea is to fast-char both sides of steak. If you do not like food that is spicy-hot with pepper, reduce amount of pepper in blackening spice.

INGREDIENTS

3 tablespoons paprika

2 teaspoons salt

1 teaspoon garlic powder

1 teaspoon onion powder

½ tablespoon black pepper

½ teaspoon white pepper

½ teaspoon oregano

1½ teaspoons cayenne pepper

4 to 6 boneless venison round or loin chop steaks, cut 1 inch thick

Butter, melted

1 Combine all spices in a blender and grind them fine to make blackening spice.

2 Heat a cast-iron skillet or griddle as hot as possible.

3 Dip venison into melted butter. Sprinkle blackening spice on both sides of venison.

4 Place venison in hot skillet; turn when it is half done and cook other side. Cook to no more than rare to medium rare.

SERVES 4 TO 6

Broiled Steak Leopold

A variation of a circa 1790 beef steak recipe named after King Leopold I of Belgium.

Salt

1 venison top round steak, cut 1½ inches thick

Fresh ground black pepper

1½ tablespoons real butter, softened

½ ounce hot brandy

1 Heat oven to broil. Salt 1 side of steak and grind on a generous portion of pepper. Press into steak. Turn steak over and repeat on other side.

2 Broil steak on both sides to rare or not more than medium rare (138° to 140°).

3 Spread butter over top of steak; return to oven until butter just begins to melt.

4 Remove steak, pour over with hot brandy and serve immediately.

SERVES 2 TO 4

Butter Grilled Round Steaks

INGREDIENTS

Venison round steak, cut 1 inch or more thick

Italian salad dressing

Salt

Pepper

Garlic powder

Onion powder

50/50 mix soy or teriyaki sauce and melted real butter

1 Soak steaks at least 4 hours in salad dressing. Remove steaks and discard marinade.

2 Season steaks with salt, pepper, garlic and onion powders.

3 Grill or broil until no more than medium rare. Baste frequently with soy sauce-butter mixture.

Philadelphia-Style Scrapple

1½ pounds venison bone-in round steaks, cut ¾ to 1 inch thick

¼ pound pork chops with bones and fat

1 quart plus 1 cup water, divided

1 white onion, sliced

1 bay leaf

1 cup white cornmeal

2 teaspoons salt

¼ cup minced onion

¼ teaspoon thyme

1 teaspoon sage

¼ teaspoon pepper

All-purpose flour

Lard or vegetable shortening

1 Combine venison, pork, 1 quart water, sliced onion and bay leaf in a large pan or pot. Cover and simmer 1 hour. Drain and reserve liquid. Discard any bones and chop meat fine.

2 Mix cornmeal, remaining 1 cup water, salt and 2 cups reserved cooking liquid in a large saucepan. Cook and stir until thickened.

3 Stir in meats, minced onion, thyme, sage and pepper. Cover and simmer 1 hour.

4 Pour into a 9x5-inch loaf pan and chill until firm, about 6 hours.

5 Cut into slices, dust lightly with flour and fry in lard until browned on both sides. Serve at once.

SERVES 6

Round Steak and Stewed Tomatoes

1 pound venison round steak, cut ¾ inch thick

3 slices bacon, chopped

1 (16-ounce) can stewed tomatoes, drained, reserving juice

½ cup chopped onion

1 teaspoon chili powder

¾ teaspoon salt

½ teaspoon paprika

¼ teaspoon pepper

Cooked rice for 2 to 4

1 Beat venison steak with sharp edge of a knife to tenderize.

2 Fry chopped bacon until it is crisp. Add steak and gently brown on both sides.

3 Reduce heat and add juice of stewed tomatoes; cover and simmer over low heat 1 hour.

4 Add stewed tomatoes, onion, chili powder, salt, paprika and pepper and simmer 1 more hour or until venison is tender. Gently stir to prevent sticking.

5 Serve with cooked rice.

SERVES 2 TO 4

Buttermilk-Soaked Round Steak

INGREDIENTS

1 cup buttermilk

¼ cup water

2 pounds venison round steak,
   cut ½ to ¾ inch thick

1 teaspoon salt

½ teaspoon black pepper

1 cup all-purpose flour

Canola or other vegetable oil

Cooked rice for 2 to 4 servings

1 Mix together buttermilk and water. Marinate steaks in buttermilk mixture 4 to 6 hours in refrigerator. Remove steaks, allow to drain and sprinkle with salt and pepper.

2 Tenderize steaks with a tenderizing mallet and dredge in flour. Add ½ inch canola oil to a hot skillet and fry steaks to rare to medium rare; turn only once.

3 Remove all but a small amount of oil and make gravy with remaining flour.

4 Serve with cooked rice and gravy.

SERVES 2 TO 4

Skillet Venison
with Simmered Vegetables

All-purpose flour

Salt

Pepper

**1 large venison round steak,
cut ¾ inch or more thick**

Vegetable oil

3 stalks celery, chopped

½ green bell pepper, chopped

3 large onions, chopped

**1 cup fresh tomatoes, skinned
and quartered**

1 Season flour with salt and pepper and pound into steak.

2 In a large heavy skillet quickly brown steak in vegetable oil.

3 Add celery, bell peppers, onions and tomatoes. Cover and cook over low heat until venison is tender (about 1¼ hours). Add a little water if needed.

SERVES 2 TO 4

Broiled Steaks with Bacon Strips

Nonstick cooking spray

**1-inch-thick venison round or
loin steaks**

Butter, melted

Lime juice

Bacon strips

1 Spray broiler pan with nonstick cooking spray. Preheat pan in oven. Baste venison steaks with butter and lime juice.

2 Place steaks in broiling pan and cover steaks with bacon strips. Broil steaks approximately 5 to 7 minutes.

3 Turn steaks, baste and lay on more bacon strips. Broil approximately 5 to 7 minutes for medium rare to medium to desired doneness.

The Remembered Piece

If the deer camp experience can be defined by a single recipe, then that recipe has to be chicken-fried venison loin steak.

I do not think that I have ever visited a deer camp where this recipe was not served—more often than not for both breakfast and dinner. The trick to cooking a perfect tenderized loin steak is to use a tool to tenderize the meat and not overcook it. These little steaks should be cooked until the blood ceases to run but with the centers still pink.

If hunting for a wall-hanging trophy is what makes me get up at 4:00 a.m., then what makes me sit in the cold and sleet in the evening and what makes me slosh through ankle-deep mud is the loin. It is the loins that are always remembered. I may be given a package or two of venison sausage or several pounds of ground venison meat. A friend may even occasionally give me a hindquarter. But I would never expect a friend, even a good friend, to give me a loin and I would not give them a venison loin either.

There are just so many things that can be done with a venison loin. They can be tied and oven roasted whole. They can be thick-cut and either broiled or grilled. They can be cooked and then sliced thin for a salad or large-cubed and used for shish kabobs. Loin steaks can be wrapped in bacon and broiled like a filet mignon and they can be used in stews and as slow-cooked roasts. There are few calls to which a venison loin will not answer.

Years ago, I was scolded by my granddad for grinding several loins into venison burger and for making several others into jerky. "Harold, Jr.," he asked, "Would you make burger and jerky from a beef T-bone steak?"

"Well, I suppose that I would not," I replied.

In those years when I get lucky and harvest more deer than usual, I use the extra loins to make jerky and burgers. In these instances, I am sure wherever granddad is now sitting that he would not scold me.

I am frequently asked, "What is your favorite venison recipe?" I don't really have a single favorite recipe. What I do have is a favorite cut of venison and a favorite technique to cook it. I like to take a 12- to 14-inch section of loin, tie it every inch or so with cotton twine, and roast it at 350° until a meat thermometer reaches 138°. I remove the loin from the oven, wrap it in aluminum foil and allow it to rest 10 to 15 minutes. I then slice it in 1½-inch-thick slices and serve it with a drool of a fruit-based sauce. This method of cooking venison loin is simple and Miss Anne does not have but one pot to wash.

There are times at deer camp when I crave something a little different, just for variety or even a special meal. These venison loin recipes will provide you with a variety of ways to prepare and serve your venison loin at camp that you may have never tried before.

LOIN

Sautéed Steak Elizabeth

6 tablespoons butter, divided

¼ cup chopped white onion

¾ cup canned beef broth

3 tablespoons dry red wine

1 tablespoon sugar

1 teaspoon pepper

8 venison loin steaks, cut ¾ inch thick

¼ cup brandy

Green onion stems, chopped

1 Melt 3 tablespoons butter in a hot skillet and add white onion. Sauté until onion just begin to brown.

2 Add broth, wine and sugar. Simmer over low heat until liquid is reduced by half and set aside.

3 Rub pepper into steaks. Melt remaining 3 tablespoons butter in a skillet. Add loin steaks and cook on medium heat to rare to medium rare. Turn only once. Remove steaks to serving plates and keep warm.

4 Remove skillet from stove and pour in brandy. Return skillet to stove and gently heat.

5 Remove skillet from stove again and ignite brandy. Let sauce stand until flames subside.

6 Add white onion mixture to skillet and bring to a boil over medium heat.

7 Spoon sauce over steaks and serve. Garnish with green onion stems.

SERVES 4 TO 6

Salisbury-Style Steaks

INGREDIENTS

¼ cup safflower or other cooking oil

6 venison loin steaks, cut ½ inch thick

2 large onions, cut thin

2 (14-ounce) cans whole tomatoes, undrained

Salt and pepper to taste

Worcestershire sauce

Mashed potatoes for 3 to 4

1 Pour oil into a hot skillet and brown steaks to just rare or medium rare on both sides. Do not overcook.

2 Add remaining ingredients except mashed potatoes, cover and simmer over medium heat 30 to 45 minutes.

3 Serve over mashed potatoes.

SERVES 3 TO 4

Flattened Steaks

INGREDIENTS

Venison loin steaks, cut ¾ to 1 inch thick

Wax paper

Salt and pepper to taste

Instant Béarnaise sauce or brown gravy

Parsley sprigs or green onion stems, chopped

1 Place loin steaks between wax paper and flatten with a mallet until ¼ inch thick.

2 Heat skillet. Add steaks and keep shaking pan so that steaks do not stick. Add a little salt and pepper while cooking. Turn just once. Do not overcook.

3 Serve hot with instant Béarnaise sauce or a milk and flour brown gravy. Garnish with chopped parsley or green onion.

Butterflied Venison Steaks

How to butterfly a loin steak: 1 inch from the end of the loin, slice across and down three-quarters of the way. Move the knife 1 inch further back and slice all the way through. Fold the two sides out to make a larger steak.

INGREDIENTS

6 venison loin steaks, cut 1½ inches thick

2 eggs

¾ cup buttermilk

1 cup all-purpose flour

Pepper and salt to taste

¼ cup butter, softened

Steak sauce

1 Butterfly loin steaks. Whisk together eggs and buttermilk and set aside. Place flour in a paper bag and season with pepper and salt.

2 Dip steaks in egg and buttermilk mixture. Place steaks, 2 at a time, in bag and shake to cover with seasoned flour.

3 Melt butter over medium-high heat and sauté venison on both sides to no more than rare to medium rare.

4 Serve with steak sauce.

SERVES 4 TO 6

Chicken-Fried Steak
with Venison Sausage Gravy

Vegetable oil, shortening or
  skillet drippings

1 egg, beaten

½ cup milk

1 cup all-purpose flour

1 teaspoon pepper

1 teaspoon salt

1 teaspoon paprika

¼ teaspoon garlic powder

¼ teaspoon poultry seasoning

2 pounds tenderized venison
  loin steak

Boiled rice for 4

VENISON SAUSAGE GRAVY:

½ to 1 pound venison breakfast
  sausage

¼ cup all-purpose flour

½ teaspoon salt

⅛ teaspoon pepper

2½ to 3 cups warm milk

1 Heat ½ inch of oil on a large skillet. In
a bowl, mix egg and milk. In a second
bowl, sift flour and all dry seasonings.

2 Roll 1 steak at a time in flour with 1
hand. With other hand, dip into egg
mixture. With first hand, roll steak in
flour a second time. This may seen like
a lot of hand swapping, but if you do it
this way, your hands stay clean.

3 Fry steaks in hot skillet until just brown
on both sides. Do not overcook.

4 Drain steaks on paper towels and serve
with boiled rice and Venison Sausage
Gravy.

VENISON SAUSAGE GRAVY:

5 Fry sausage and drain and crumble.
Reserve ¼ cup of drippings in skillet
and heat over medium heat.

6 Dissolve flour, salt and pepper into milk.
Gradually add milk mixture to skillet
and stir constantly. Keep stirring until
gravy begins to thicken. Stir in sausage
and serve.

SERVES 4

Chicken-Fried Steak

INGREDIENTS

CHICKEN-FRIED STEAK SEASONING:

1 teaspoon ground oregano

1 teaspoon ground sage

1 teaspoon dried basil

1 teaspoon dried marjoram

1 teaspoon chili powder

1 teaspoon onion salt

1 teaspoon garlic powder

1 teaspoon black pepper

1 tablespoon Ac'cent (MSG)

2 teaspoons salt

2 tablespoons paprika

STEAK:

Tenderized venison steaks

Eggs, beaten

All-purpose flour

Safflower oil or other cooking oil

1 cup cold milk or more if needed

Salt and pepper to taste

Cooked white rice

1. Mix spices and place in a shaker. Sprinkle tenderized venison steaks with seasoning on both sides.

2. Place beaten eggs in a bowl and flour in another bowl. With one hand, dip individual steaks in egg, transfer to flour. With other hand, cover and press on flour. Continue until all steaks are floured.

3. Fry steaks in hot oil until almost medium (still slightly pink inside); do not overcook.

4. Pour off all but 1 tablespoon cooking oil and scrape browned bits from bottom of skillet.

5. Whisk 1 tablespoon flour into cold milk and stir into skillet with drippings and browned bits. Stir constantly until gravy begins to thicken; stir in more cold milk if needed. Salt and pepper to taste.

6. Serve gravy over steaks and cooked rice.

Fried Cutlets
with Sour Cream Sauce

INGREDIENTS

1 cup all-purpose flour

Salt and pepper to taste

2 tablespoons sugar

2 pounds bone-in loin cutlets,
  cut ½ inch thick

2 tablespoons butter

½ cup sour cream

Worcestershire sauce

Celery salt

1 bay leaf

1 Sift together flour, salt, pepper and sugar and dredge cutlets.

2 Melt butter in a skillet and brown cutlets.

3 Season sour cream with salt, pepper, Worcestershire sauce, celery salt and bay leaf and pour over cutlets.

4 Cover skillet and simmer over very low heat 45 minutes to 1 hour or until venison is tender. Remove bay leaf before serving.

SERVES 6 TO 8

J. My Favorite Hunting Bud
and Her First Buck

Mexican-Style Venison Loin

- ¾ teaspoon chili powder
- ½ teaspoon garlic powder
- ½ teaspoon pepper
- ¼ teaspoon salt
- ¼ teaspoon dried oregano
- ¼ teaspoon ground cumin
- 4 venison loin steaks, cut 1 inch thick
- 1 teaspoon canola or other vegetable cooking oil
- ½ cup canned beef broth
- ¼ cup balsamic or other mild vinegar, such as rice wine vinegar
- 2 tablespoons jalapeño or other red pepper jelly

1 Combine chili powder, garlic powder, pepper, salt, oregano and cumin; mix well. Rub chili powder mixture into all sides of steaks.

2 Heat oil in a skillet over medium-high heat. Add steaks and cook 3 minutes on each side. Do not overcook. Remove steaks from skillet, set aside and keep warm.

3 Add broth, vinegar and jelly to skillet and cook 5 minutes or until slightly reduced, stirring frequently. Spoon sauce over steaks.

SERVES 2 TO 4

Poached Filet of Venison
with Horseradish Sauce

**1½ pounds venison loin,
trimmed**

Cotton twine

1 clove garlic, slivered

1 quart canned beef broth

**2 teaspoons prepared creamy
horseradish**

1 teaspoon fresh lemon juice

3 ounces butter, softened

1 Tie twine around loin every 1 to 2
inches. Make small cuts and insert garlic
slivers.

2 Place broth in a large pan and bring to a
boil. Lay in loin and simmer until 138°
to 140° internal temperature is reached.
Remove venison, cover and let it rest
while you make sauce.

3 Pour ¾ cup of broth into a small pan
and reduce until about ¼ cup remains.
Remove reduced broth from stove. Add
horseradish and lemon juice and whisk
in butter gradually to achieve a creamy
consistency.

4 Remove twine from venison, slice it
and place on a serving platter. Pour a
little horseradish sauce over and serve
remainder of sauce separately.

SERVES 4

Filet Mignon-Style Venison Loin Steaks

Courtesy of Mr. James "Blimp" Curtis.

INGREDIENTS

8- to 10-inch venison loin, cut from large end

8 pieces thick-cut rindless smoked bacon

8 natural wooden toothpicks

Salt and pepper to taste

1 Slice loin into 1-inch-thick filets. Wrap a piece of bacon around edge of each filet and secure with a toothpick. Sprinkle with salt and pepper.

2 Broil on 1 side for 3 to 5 minutes. Turn over and broil another 3 to 5 minutes. Cook to no more than medium rare.

SERVES 4 TO 8

Braised Venison Loin
with Lime and Hot Peppers

INGREDIENTS

4 pounds venison loin, cut into small bite-size pieces

1 onion, chopped

2 tablespoons crushed red pepper

4 garlic cloves, minced

1 tablespoon fresh lime juice

⅔ cup soy sauce

3 tablespoons brown sugar

Cooked rice for 6 to 8

1 In saucepan or deep skillet, sauté venison, onion, red pepper and garlic over high heat until just browned.

2 Add lime juice, soy sauce and brown sugar. Reduce heat, cover and simmer about 10 minutes.

3 Serve over cooked rice.

SERVES 6 TO 8

Filet Mignon-Style Venison Loin Steaks

Uncle Melvin's Venison Biscuits and Molasses

These biscuits are easy to make and are great for hunters to carry in their pockets on a cool fall morning. Written especially for Melvin Tingle.

INGREDIENTS

Venison loin, cut ¼ inch thick

Chicken-Fried Steak Seasoning (page 38)

Vegetable shortening

2 to 2½ cups plus 2 to 4 tablespoons self-rising flour, divided

½ cup lard or vegetable shortening

1 cup buttermilk

Butter, softened

Sorghum or other molasses

Salt and pepper to taste

1 Preheat oven to 475°. Rub loin slices with steak seasoning and place in refrigerator until biscuits are done.

2 Grease a baking sheet with shortening. Place 2 to 2½ cups flour into large bowl and make a crater in center of flour. Add lard and buttermilk and work mixture with your finger tips until dough is soft and sticky.

3 Place dough on floured surface and sift a little of remaining flour on top. Knead dough just enough until it is no longer sticky. Do not overknead. Roll flat to ¾ inch or more thick. Cut with a cookie cutter; do not twist. Place biscuits, with edges touching, on baking sheet. Bake 8 minutes or until tops are brown.

4 Open biscuits, place a pad of butter inside, close biscuit and allow butter to melt. Very quickly sauté loin slices in butter until just barely browned. Do not overcook.

5 Reopen biscuits and add cooked loin and pour on a little sorghum. Salt and pepper to taste. Wrap each biscuit in aluminum foil or plastic wrap.

Cranberry Marinated Kabobs

1 cup cranberry juice

¼ cup olive oil

1 teaspoon minced garlic

½ teaspoon onion salt

½ teaspoon celery salt

½ teaspoon pepper

½ teaspoon sweet basil

¼ teaspoon ginger

2 pounds venison loin, cubed 2 inches or more thick

Wooden skewers

Mushroom caps

Pearl onions

Green bell peppers, cut into 2-inch pieces

Cherry tomatoes

1 Mix together cranberry juice, olive oil, garlic, onion salt, celery salt, pepper, basil and ginger. Pour into a 1-gallon zip-close bag.

2 Add venison and marinate in refrigerator 8 hours or overnight.

3 Soak wooden skewers in water 1 hour before using. Preheat grill to high.

4 Drain venison cubes and reserve marinade. Bring reserved marinade to a full boil then set aside to cool.

5 Alternate venison and vegetables on skewers and grill for a few minutes. Baste with boiled marinade several times while cooking. Cook quickly to not more than medium rare. Do not overcook.

SERVES 4 TO 6

The Forgotten Piece

The Forgotten Piece is an appropriate title for this section because the tenderloin is sometimes forgotten. As many folks that have used my skinning shed, gut pile, meat saw, knife sharpener, propane heater, and water to wash their deer over the years, few have ever offered me a loin or even a piece of loin. But, what they have offered me were their diminutive little tenderloins and for this I am very grateful.

My idea of hunting at a deer camp is to spend time at a rustic, traditional deer camp that was once a remote homestead used by successive generations as their gathering place. Some say that I may be a romantic. I may well be a romantic, and like this old hunting camp, we both may also be vestiges of the past. Not as many of these old camps are around today as there were in the 1950's. Some still exist and like a measurable number of my fellow senior citizen hunters, we think these old deer camps should be maintained and saved for future generations.

I have told this venison tenderloin story many times before, but it is worth the retelling. I once knew an ol' hunter who hunted at one of these old family camps. Two of the things I remember about him were his red-checked wool shirt and his knee-high, lace-up leather boots. I have no idea how old he, his shirt or his boots were, but he was old and from what I knew of him, his shirt and boots could have been handed down to him from several previous generations.

Besides his vintage shirt and boots, there was one other thing I remember about him. The only meat he ever wanted from each deer was one tenderloin—and that was all. Other hunters would carry home an ice chest full of hindquarters and loins, but not he. One day I asked him why it was that all he ever wanted from each deer was one little tenderloin. He said, "Don't you know? I'm a country fellow and all these other folks live in the city. I know what eats good and they wouldn't know the best eatin' part of a deer if it landed in their lap."

Tenderloins—Small But Full of Flavor

If you have ever enjoyed a beef filet mignon or the small piece of meat in a beef T-bone steak, you were eating tenderloin. No one has to tell you the best part of a T-bone steak is the small part. For some reason, most hunters have never equated a filet mignon or a T-bone steak with a deer. When I am offered the tenderloins, I stand there with my eyes looking down, my hand out, and mumble a muffled, "Thank you very much" just as if they are doing me no favor. At the same time I am smiling inside.

I remember to this day one of the biggest mistakes I ever made at a deer camp. Back in the mid-1980's, I hunted with a group of folks that were really "mad at the deer" that year. By mid-season, they had already harvested eleven deer and had given me sixteen tenderloins. Although my hunting luck was nowhere as good as theirs, I was grateful I had been invited to hunt. On the last night, I brought out several of my tenderloins and cooked them a fine dinner. From that point forward, not a single tenderloin came my way. I learned my lesson well. Today, every time I am given an "embarrassingly small" tenderloin, I keep my mouth shut.

Yes, a tenderloin is small, but each deer has two of them and two are all I need for a fine dinner. One of my favorite ways to cook venison tenderloins is to cut them into 1-inch long sections and gently and quickly sauté them in a skillet. Sautéing gives me the opportunity to press the meat with my finger. When the surface just begins to firm, it is cooked to medium rare and perfectly done.

TENDERLOIN

Tenderloin of Venison Tartare

If you have ever enjoyed Steak Tartare, you will recognize this dish and you will remember how much you had to pay for it in that up-scale restaurant. Besides having one's face bloodied after taking their first deer, I know of one camp where the honoree must dine on tenderloin tartare.

INGREDIENTS

- 1 pound fresh venison tenderloin, ground twice through a fine disc
- 1 very small egg (chicken, Banny hen or quail)
- 1 green onion, minced
- 1 tablespoon capers
- ¼ teaspoon prepared French mustard
- 1 teaspoon minced parsley
- 1 teaspoon Worcestershire sauce
- Salt and freshly ground pepper to taste

1 Press ground venison into a ramekin (small glass ovenproof bowl). Invert and unmold ramekin onto center of a serving plate.

2 Press a small well in center and break a raw egg into it. Garnish with onion, capers, mustard and parsley. Season to taste with Worcestershire sauce and salt and pepper.

3 May also serve as an appetizer when spread on thin toasted bread rounds.

Chicken-Fried Tenderloin

3 to 4 venison tenderloins

2 cups all-purpose flour

⅛ teaspoon black pepper

½ teaspoon garlic powder

½ teaspoon paprika

½ teaspoon thyme

½ teaspoon lemon pepper

Pinch cayenne pepper

½ cup whole milk

½ cup buttermilk

Canola oil

4 fresh deseeded jalapeño
peppers, charbroiled

LEMON WHITE SAUCE:

2 tablespoons butter

1½ to 2 tablespoons all-purpose
flour

1 cup half-and-half or milk

1 teaspoon lemon juice

1 teaspoon sherry

1 Cut venison tenderloin into 1-inch-long pieces and pound to tenderize.

2 Mix flour and seasonings in a bowl. Mix milk and buttermilk in a second bowl. Dip tenderloin first in flour mixture, then into milk mixture and back into flour mixture.

3 Quickly sauté tenderloins in medium-hot canola oil until browned on each side and cooked to no more than medium rare.

4 Serve with Lemon Flavored White Sauce and charbroiled jalapeño peppers.

LEMON WHITE SAUCE:

5 Melt butter over low heat. Slowly sift in flour and stir 3 to 4 minutes.

6 Slowly stir in half-and-half. Simmer and whisk until sauce is thickened. When sauce begins to boil, add lemon juice and sherry.

SERVES 4

Slow-Cooked Tenderloin
with Italian Tomatoes

INGREDIENTS

3 slices bacon, chopped

1 pound tenderloin, cut across the grain ½ inch thick

1 (16-ounce) can Italian-style stewed tomatoes, undrained and divided

¾ cup chopped onion

½ teaspoon chili powder

½ teaspoon oregano

¾ teaspoon salt

½ teaspoon paprika

¼ teaspoon pepper

Cooked angel hair spaghetti for 2 to 4

1 Fry bacon until crisp. Add tenderloin and gently brown on all sides. Do not overcook.

2 To a slow cooker, add venison, bacon, juice of stewed tomatoes, onion, chili powder, oregano, salt, paprika and pepper. Cook on low 5 hours.

3 Add stewed tomatoes and cook 1 hour more. Serve on angel hair spaghetti.

SERVES 2 TO 4

Bacon Wrapped and Broiled Butterflied Medallions

Courtesy, Mr. James "Blimp" Curtis

INGREDIENTS

2 venison tenderloins

½ pound thick-cut skinless bacon strips

2 (8-ounce) bottles Wishbone Italian Salad Dressing

Natural wooden toothpicks

1 Cut tenderloins across grain into 2-inch long pieces. Center knife on each piece and slice across grain three quarters of the way through. Lay open to make butterfly medallions.

2 Divide butterflied medallions and dressing into several zip-close plastic bags and refrigerate 1 hour. Remove venison from marinade and reserve liquid.

3 Wrap a piece of bacon around each butterflied medallion and secure with a toothpick. Broil as you would a small filet mignon. Be careful not to overcook; these small medallions cook very quickly. Cook to no more than medium rare.

SERVES 2 TO 4

Cajun-Fried "Little-Snakes"

4 venison tenderloins

3 cups milk

½ teaspoon garlic juice

1 teaspoon paprika

½ teaspoon onion powder

½ teaspoon cayenne pepper

¼ teaspoon black pepper

Salt to taste

½ cup all-purpose flour

⅛ teaspoon white pepper

⅛ teaspoon oregano

⅛ teaspoon rosemary

Cotton string

1 cup vegetable shortening

Cooked mashed potatoes for 4 to 6

Brown gravy for 4 to 6

Corn on cob for 4 to 6

Coleslaw for 4 to 6

1 Cover tenderloins with milk and garlic juice in a plastic mixing bowl or zip-close plastic bag and refrigerate overnight.

2 Drain tenderloins and pat dry; season with paprika, onion powder, cayenne, black pepper and salt.

3 Mix together flour, white pepper, oregano and rosemary. Dredge venison in seasoned flour.

4 Coil each tenderloin and tie with cotton string. Dredge venison a second time.

5 Heat shortening in a skillet. Fry tenderloins until golden brown.

6 Remove strings and serve whole with mashed potatoes, brown gravy, corn on cob and coleslaw.

SERVES 4 TO 6

Real Deer Hunters Do Eat Quiche

1 venison tenderloin

Olive oil

1 (9-inch) frozen pie shell, thawed

4 eggs, beaten

1 cup shredded Swiss cheese

1¼ cups whole milk

½ teaspoon salt

⅛ teaspoon ground nutmeg

⅛ teaspoon black pepper

½ (15-ounce) can asparagus pieces, drained

1 Rub tenderloin with olive oil and quickly broil or grill to no more than rare and set aside to rest.

2 Preheat oven to 450°. Place pie shell in an ovenproof glass pie plate. Brush inside of pie shell with a small amount of beaten egg. Prick bottom and sides of pie shell with a fork and bake 5 minutes or until light golden brown.

3 Slice venison into thin slices across grain. Mix together sliced venison and shredded cheese and place in pie shell.

4 Mix and beat together remainder of beaten eggs, milk, salt, nutmeg and pepper. Stir in asparagus pieces and pour over venison and cheese.

5 Bake 35 to 40 minutes or until a knife inserted near center comes out clean.

6 Remove from oven and let stand 10 minutes before serving.

SERVES 4 TO 6

GROUND VENISON

Keeping It Fresh

I have no idea how many pounds of ground venison I have seen consumed at deer camps and I have been one of the leading consumers. In my opinion, the main reason so much ground venison is eaten at deer camp is because it is so versatile, so easy to cook and most of us have an ample supply in the freezer to bring along with us.

Since most recipes call for ground venison in one-pound increments, most venison processors now package their ground venison in plastic one-pound bags. Ground meat stays much fresher and for a longer period of time in the vacuum-sealed plastic bags than it did in the traditional paper wrapping, and when packaged in one-pound lots, there is no waste. If you need more ground venison for a recipe, just thaw several packages. The safest way to thaw ground venison or any meat or vegetable is to place the frozen package in the refrigerator and allow it to thaw slowly.

The Taste Test

I was once guilty of submerging my raw deer meat in ice water for several days before taking it to the processor. Why? For no reason other than someone told me I should. One day I began to wonder if I was doing myself a favor or whether I was harming my hard-earned harvest. Since I would never consider doing this with expensive grocery store beef, I wondered what effect soaking has on the quality of the meat. So I did an experiment with two hindquarters from the same deer.

First, I weighed both hindquarters and then placed one in an ice chest, covered it with ice, and let it sit for two days. I sealed the other hindquarter in two layers of plastic bags, placed it into an ice chest, and covered it with ice.

After two days, the hindquarter that had been covered directly with ice and "soaked" had turned white, had gained 4.5% of its original weight, and the water had infiltrated ½ inch deep into the flesh.

The hindquarter sealed in plastic bags was red and weighed the same as it did when it was placed in the cooler.

Hindquarter soaked turned gray after two days

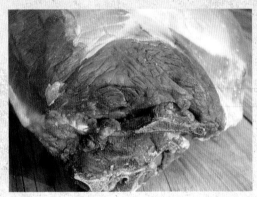

Hindquarter sealed in plastic bags stayed red

To determine if I could taste a difference, I cut the same steak from each hindquarter and made several pounds of venison burger and sausage from each. I could definitely tell the difference between the two hindquarters. The sealed meat tasted fresh and more like beef.

I also did a blind taste test with a friend. He found the sausage made from the soaked meat did not taste quite as good as the sausage made from the unsoaked meat. He definitely did not like the taste of the steak or the burger that was made from the soaked meat. He said they did not have as much flavor, tasted bland, and the steak had a mushy texture.

I began to think, "How can I cool and transport it without it absorbing water and losing its natural flavor?"

GROUND VENISON

How to Store Fresh Venison

If you need to keep your harvest cool for several days while driving back home, the solution to the problem is simple and inexpensive. I remembered how my mom would ice-down and transport her raw turkey and cooked ham for the two-day drive to grandmother's house for Thanksgiving and Christmas. Her feasts always arrived just as fresh as when we left home.

1. Seal your raw game meat in two plastic bags, one plastic bag inside of the other.
2. Place the double-sealed bags into your ice chest.
3. Then fill the chest with ice.

Packaged in this manner, your game will remain cool, it will not absorb water, and the natural taste and texture will be preserved.

Baked Corn, Potatoes and Ground Venison

INGREDIENTS

1 pound ground venison burger, cooked

1 (15-ounce) can cream-style corn

2 tablespoons butter or margarine, melted

8 Cheddar or other cheese slices

4 cups cooked mashed potatoes

1 (10-count) tube canned biscuits

1 Preheat oven to 350°. Spread cooked venison on bottom of a 9x13-inch ovenproof casserole dish.

2 Spread creamed corn over venison. Pour melted butter over corn. Cover with cheese slices. Spread mashed potatoes over cheese slices.

3 Place canned biscuits on top of potatoes. You may need to gently stretch biscuits so they cover entire surface of dish. Bake until hot, bubbly and biscuits are done and brown.

SERVES 4 TO 6

Corn, Kidney Bean and Venison Casserole

1 pound ground venison burger

4 celery stalks, diced

2 medium onions, chopped

1 (10.75-ounce) can tomato soup

1 (15-ounce) can cream-style corn

1 (15-ounce) can kidney beans, drained

1 clove garlic, minced

Pepper to taste

1½ tablespoons Worcestershire sauce

1 teaspoon chili sauce

1 (9.75-ounce) package corn chips, crushed

1 Preheat oven to 375°. In a skillet, brown venison; add celery and onions and cook 3 minutes stirring occasionally.

2 Reduce heat and add tomato soup, corn, beans, garlic, pepper, Worcestershire and chili sauce. Pour venison mixture into a 2-quart casserole dish and bake uncovered 20 minutes.

3 Cover with corn chips and bake another 10 to 15 minutes or until chips are slightly toasted.

SERVES 8

Egg Noodles and Venison Dinner

INGREDIENTS

½ pound ground venison

Vegetable oil

½ medium onion, chopped

½ green bell pepper, chopped

1 cup canned tomatoes

½ teaspoon Worcestershire sauce

½ teaspoon salt

¹⁄₁₆ teaspoon pepper

¾ cup water

3 ounces uncooked egg noodles

1 Gently brown ground venison in vegetable oil. Add onion and green pepper and continue cooking until onion is lightly brown.

2 Add tomatoes, Worcestershire, salt, pepper and water. Stir and heat to boiling.

3 Spread uncooked noodles on top of venison mixture. Cover and simmer 15 minutes or until noodles have absorbed liquid.

SERVES 2 TO 4

Three-Cheese Baked Lasagna

INGREDIENTS

4 tablespoons olive oil

¾ pound ground venison round steak

½ pound spicy venison link sausage, skinned and sliced ¼ inch thick

2 onions, chopped fine

2 cloves garlic, minced

1 (14-ounce) can Italian tomatoes, coarsely chopped

2 (8-ounce) cans tomato sauce

3 tablespoons sugar

1 tablespoon salt

1 tablespoon chopped fresh oregano

1 tablespoon chopped fresh basil

1½ cups grated Parmesan cheese, divided

¼ teaspoon pepper

½ pound dry lasagna noodles

Salt to taste

2 tablespoons olive or vegetable oil

1 pound ricotta cheese, sliced

1 pound mozzarella cheese, grated

1 Heat olive oil in a heavy saucepan. Add steak and sausage and sauté until just browned.

2 Add onions and garlic and sauté 3 minutes more. Add tomatoes, tomato sauce, sugar, salt, oregano, basil, ½ cup Parmesan cheese and pepper. Mix well. Bring to a boil, reduce heat and simmer slowly 2 hours, stirring occasionally.

3 When sauce is almost finished, fill a large pot with water. Add salt and 2 tablespoons oil. Bring to a boil and add lasagna noodles 2 at a time. Let water come to a boil again after each addition. Simmer 15 minutes and drain.

4 Preheat oven to 350°. In bottom of a greased 9x13-inch baking dish spread a thin layer of sauce, then a layer of pasta and then a layer of cheeses. Repeat these layers twice, ending with a layer of sauce. Sprinkle with remaining Parmesan cheese.

5 Bake 40 minutes and let stand 15 minutes before serving.

SERVES 8

Green Chile Cheese Pie

2 tablespoons canola or safflower oil

1 large onion, chopped

1 pound ground venison

1 teaspoon salt

¼ cup chopped canned green chiles

⅛ teaspoon oregano

1 (8-ounce) can tomato sauce

2 cups biscuit mix, mixed per directions on package

All-purpose flour

½ cup shredded sharp Cheddar cheese

1 Preheat oven to 425°. Heat oil in a skillet and cook onions until they are just clear.

2 Add ground venison, salt, green chiles and oregano. Cook until venison is just brown, drain and place in an ovenproof dish.

3 Add tomato sauce and place in oven as it preheats until dough is prepared.

4 Pat biscuit dough out on a floured board into a 10-inch circle. Cut dough into wedges and lay on top of venison filling. Bake 15 to 20 minutes or until dough is brown.

5 Lay a flat pan on top; turn over to remove. Sprinkle with shredded cheese.

6 Place under broiler a few minutes to melt cheese.

SERVES 6

Vegetable Pie

1½ pounds ground venison

1 medium onion, chopped

1 clove garlic, chopped

3 tablespoons safflower oil

2 cups plus ¼ cup water, divided

2 tablespoons Worcestershire sauce

1 teaspoon marjoram

1 teaspoon thyme

1 teaspoon celery seed

1 bay leaf, halved

1 teaspoon salt

½ teaspoon pepper

1 pound peeled and diced raw potatoes

1 carrot, diced

2 tablespoons all-purpose flour

½ cup fresh or frozen English peas

2 (8-inch) prepared pie crusts

1 Sauté ground venison, onion and garlic in oil.

2 Transfer to a large pot and add 2 cups water, Worcestershire sauce, herbs, salt and pepper. Bring to a boil and simmer 30 minutes.

3 Add potatoes and carrot; cook 20 minutes more. Remove bay leaf.

4 Whisk flour into ¼ cup water and slowly stir into pot. Bring to a gentle boil and cook until mixture thickens. Add peas. Remove from heat, cover and set aside.

5 Preheat oven to 450°. Line bottom of a pie pan with 1 pie crust. Pour meat mixture into pie pan.

6 Cut decorative slits in second pie crust and gently place on top. Crimp edges to seal. Bake until crust is browned.

SERVES 4 TO 6

Pachongas

A variation of a Mexican rolled flour tortilla recipe.

6 pounds ground venison burger

2 tablespoons cooking oil

4 large onions, chopped

4 green onions, chopped

4 green bell peppers, chopped

4 red chiles, sliced (optional)

36 flour tortillas

24 ounces Colby cheese, shredded

12 ounces sharp Cheddar cheese, shredded

Corn oil

Lettuce, shredded

Tomatoes, chopped

Onions, chopped

Cheddar cheese, grated

Picante sauce

Sour cream

1 Brown venison in oil. Add onions, green onions, bell peppers and chiles. Sauté until onions are just clear. Remove and drain.

2 Place a heaping spoonful of mixture on each tortilla. Top with a spoonful of each cheese. Roll tortilla tightly and fry in corn oil until golden. Drain.

3 Place 3 Pachongas on a dinner plate and cover with a generous portion of lettuce, tomatoes, onions, Cheddar cheese, picante sauce and sour cream.

MAKES 36 PACHONGAS

Empanadas

An empanada is a savory pie indigenous to Spain.

¼ cup butter

1 pound ground venison

2 large onions, chopped

½ cup chopped green olives

½ cup chopped celery

2 jalapeño peppers, chopped
(optional)

Salt and pepper to taste

2 tablespoons apple cider
vinegar

1 (8-ounce) can tomato sauce

2 tablespoons Worcestershire
sauce

2 to 3 (8-inch) prepared pie
crusts

Shortening

1 Preheat oven to 350°. In a large skillet, melt butter and brown venison. Add remaining ingredients, except pie crusts, and simmer about 20 minutes. Remove from stove, cover and chill.

2 Cut pie crusts into 3-inch circles. Prick circles with a fork. Place venison mixture in center, fold over and seal edges.

3 Place on a greased cookie sheet and bake 20 to 25 minutes.

SERVES 4 TO 6

Mexican-Style Chile Pizza

1 pound ground venison

2 tablespoons cooking oil

¼ teaspoon salt

1 (12-inch) prebaked thick pizza crust

1 cup chunky salsa

2 cups shredded Monterey Jack cheese, divided

1 (4-ounce) can chopped green chiles, drained

3 Italian tomatoes, seeded and chopped

⅓ cup slivered red onion

2 tablespoons chopped fresh cilantro

1 Preheat oven to 450°. Brown ground venison in oil until just pink. Crumble, sprinkle with salt and set aside.

2 Place pizza crust on a large baking sheet and spread with salsa. Sprinkle over with half the shredded cheese. Cover with remaining ingredients, except cilantro. Sprinkle on remaining cheese last.

3 Bake 10 to 12 minutes or until cheese topping is melted. Sprinkle with chopped cilantro and slice.

SERVES 4

A World of Meat Balls

Back in the late 1980's when the camo, ATVs, and tree stand businesses were just beginning to take off, I lived relatively close to a tree stand builder. I had known the owner for some years and had purchased one of his first climbing tree stands. He still had his day job back then and was building his tree stands in his garage at night. He even delivered it to my home and climbed a power pole behind the house to teach me how it worked. In the

mid-1990's he was preparing to open his big factory and was having a grand opening. This was one fine plant. It had automatic welding machines, a chain track that carried the tree stands though the then state-of-the-art powder coating paint booth, and an automatic packaging machine.

For this grand opening celebration, he "invited" me to drive down and do some outdoor venison cooking for him. Since he had been kind enough to personally hand-deliver my tree stand, I could not say no. I decided to make meat balls on-site and fry them in a large

skillet on a propane burner. He was to supply the propane, the burners, the venison, and several staff to help grind the meat, mix the ingredients, and shape and cook the meat balls—and he did.

I arrived at the site of his new plant around 10:00 a.m. The grand opening was scheduled to begin at noon so I figured that two hours would be enough time for me to get set up and organize my crew of new helpers. And it was. He had no idea how many people would attend his grand opening and if I had known, I may have feigned a serious illness.

I don't know how many meat balls that we ground, mixed, and cooked that day,

Miss Anne making venison meat balls

but even cooking in batches of one hundred or so, we could not cook them fast enough. Even Miss Anne got into the act. Now you have to know something about Miss Anne to appreciate the level of this commitment. I have seen her dig in a garden with dirt up to her elbows, I have seen her baking sherry cakes with batter on her nose, but greasy hands is not something that I had ever seen before.

At the height of this meat ball making melee, I looked over one time and saw her wearing one of my camo shirts and a red apron, stuffing venison and beef trimmings in the grinder with one hand and catching the greasy ground meat with the other hand. I will not say that she had a smile on her face, but she was a real trooper. I don't know what I would have done that day if she had not pitched in—and she has never let me forget it.

If the number of venison meat balls that were consumed during that grand opening is any indication of how good venison meat balls are, then they need no more testimonials.

Quick and Easy Meat Balls

Ground venison burger can be substituted for ground beef or ground pork.

INGREDIENTS

¾ **pound ground venison**

¼ **pound ground beef or ground pork**

½ **cup stale breadcrumbs**

1 **egg, lightly beaten**

1 **(1.25-ounce) envelope dry onion soup mix, divided**

2 **tablespoons shortening**

1 Combine ground meats, breadcrumbs, egg, 2 tablespoons dry onion soup mix and just enough water to hold together. Roll into small balls and brown in melted shortening. Remove and drain.

2 Pour off shortening and return meat balls to skillet. Add remaining dry onion soup mix, cover with water and simmer over very low heat 1 hour. Add more water if needed while simmering.

SERVES 4

Slow-Cooked Beer-Flavored Meat Balls

INGREDIENTS

2 **recipes Quick and Easy Meat Balls, uncooked (above)**

2 **medium onions, quartered**

1 **(12-ounce) bottle beer**

1½ **cups ketchup**

2 **tablespoons wine vinegar**

¼ **teaspoon garlic powder**

¼ **teaspoon salt**

¼ **teaspoon pepper**

¼ **cup light brown sugar**

1 Mix all ingredients in a slow cooker and cook on low 8 hours.

SERVES 8

Venison Meat Balls
in Tomato-Vegetable Sauce

Ground venison burger can be substituted for ground beef or ground pork.

1½ pounds ground venison

½ pound ground beef or pork

2 teaspoons salt

¼ teaspoon pepper

1 onion, chopped fine

1 cup finely chopped celery

½ cup chopped green bell
pepper

4 eggs, slightly beaten

1 cup cracker crumbs

4 tablespoons cooking oil

TOMATO-VEGETABLE SAUCE:

1 cup finely chopped onion

2 garlic cloves, chopped fine

2 tablespoons olive oil

4 tablespoons butter

2 cups Italian Roma tomatoes,
peeled, seeded and chopped
or 1 (8-ounce) can seasoned
tomato sauce

1 teaspoon salt

1 teaspoon pepper

1½ teaspoons basil

3 tablespoons tomato paste

24 soft black olives, pitted

1 Mix together ground meats, salt, pepper, onion, celery, bell pepper, eggs and cracker crumbs and grind a second time. Shape mixture into small 1-inch (1 heaping tablespoon) balls and gently brown in cooking oil.

2 Pour Tomato-Vegetable Sauce over meat balls and gently simmer 45 minutes to 1 hour.

TOMATO-VEGETABLE SAUCE:

3 Sauté onion and garlic in oil and butter in a large skillet. Add remaining ingredients and simmer 20 minutes before adding meat balls.

SERVES 4

Swedish-Style Meat Balls

Ground venison burger can be substituted for ground beef or ground pork.

1 pound ground venison

½ pound ground beef or pork

½ cup instant mashed potatoes

1 cup fine dry breadcrumbs, divided

1 egg, lightly beaten

1 teaspoon salt

¼ teaspoon pepper

½ teaspoon packed dark brown sugar

¼ teaspoon ground allspice

¼ teaspoon ground nutmeg

⅛ teaspoon ground cloves

⅛ teaspoon ground ginger

3 tablespoons butter or margarine

1 Lightly mix ground meats, potatoes, ½ cup breadcrumbs, egg, salt, pepper, brown sugar, allspice, nutmeg, cloves and ginger. Shape into 1-inch balls and roll balls in remaining ½ cup breadcrumbs.

2 Heat butter in a large skillet and brown meat balls on all sides. Cover and cook about 15 minutes or until meat balls are done.

3 Makes about 3 dozen meat balls.

SERVES 6 TO 8

Spaghetti with Meat Balls
in Spicy Tomato Sauce

Ground venison burger can be substituted for ground beef or ground pork.

MEAT BALLS:

1 pound ground venison

½ pound ground beef or pork

½ cup chopped bell pepper

½ cup chopped onion

3 tablespoons minced fresh
   cilantro

1 egg, slightly beaten

¼ cup ketchup

1 teaspoon Worcestershire
   sauce

½ teaspoon salt

¼ teaspoon pepper

1 teaspoon chili powder

½ teaspoon cumin

½ teaspoon dried leaf oregano

½ teaspoon garlic powder

¾ cup unseasoned
   breadcrumbs (more or less)

TOMATO & CHILI SAUCE:

2 (14-ounce) cans Italian-style
   diced tomatoes

1 (8-ounce) can tomato sauce

¼ teaspoon hot sauce, optional

1 teaspoon chili powder

1 Preheat oven to 425°. Mix meat ball ingredients except for breadcrumbs. Slowly mix in breadcrumbs until mixture is firm. Use hands and shape mixture into 1-inch balls.

2 Place meat balls on a large cookie sheet or in a baking pan and bake 15 minutes. Turn meat balls and bake another 15 minutes.

3 Add to Tomato & Chili Sauce and simmer 20 minutes.

4 Serve over cooked spaghetti.

TOMATO & CHILI SAUCE:

5 While meat balls are cooking, heat ingredients in a small stockpot.

SERVES 6

Stove-Top Meat Balls
with Mexican Chili-Tomato Sauce

Ground venison burger can be substituted for ground beef or ground pork.

MEAT BALLS:

¾ pound ground venison

¼ pound ground beef or pork

1 clove garlic, minced

½ teaspoon crumbled oregano leaves

1 small onion, minced

1 teaspoon salt

½ teaspoon pepper

1 egg, beaten

¼ cup white cornmeal

MEXICAN CHILI-TOMATO SAUCE:

1 tablespoon margarine

1 small onion, chopped

1 garlic clove, minced

2 tablespoons chili powder

½ teaspoon cumin

¼ teaspoon crumbled oregano leaves

3 cups tomato juice

Salt to taste

MEAT BALLS:

1 Combine all meat ball ingredients and mix well. With your hands, shape 1-inch meat balls and set aside.

MEXICAN CHILI-TOMATO SAUCE:

2 Melt margarine in a saucepan or small stockpot. Add onion and cook until just clear and beginning to brown.

3 Add remaining ingredients and meat balls. Bring to a boil, lower heat to a simmer and cook until meat balls are fully cooked.

SERVES 4

Stove-Top Sweet & Sour Meat Balls

Ground venison burger can be substituted for ground beef or ground pork.

MEAT BALLS:

1 pound ground venison

½ pound ground beef or pork

½ cup milk

½ teaspoon soy sauce

1 egg, beaten

¾ cup quick oatmeal

¼ cup sliced or chopped water chestnuts

½ teaspoon garlic powder

½ teaspoon onion powder

½ teaspoon salt

Cooking oil

SWEET & SOUR SAUCE:

1 cup light brown sugar

2 tablespoons cornstarch or arrowroot

½ cup beef broth

½ cup vinegar

2 teaspoons soy sauce

½ cup coarse-chopped green bell pepper

1 (8-ounce) can pineapple pieces, drained

MEAT BALLS:

1 Mix all meat ball ingredients and use hands to shape into 1-inch meat balls.

2 Heat cooking oil in a large skillet and brown meat balls on all sides. Drain meat balls on paper towels and set aside.

SWEET & SOUR SAUCE:

3 Mix brown sugar, cornstarch, beef broth, vinegar and soy sauce in a Dutch oven or small stockpot and bring to a boil. Boil sauce mixture until it begins to thicken.

4 Stir in bell pepper, pineapple pieces and meat balls. Simmer 30 minutes. Serve over cooked white rice.

SERVES 8

Meatloaf

In every deer camp I have ever visited, whether it be a long established and rustic camp, a former share-cropper's house, a 1950's-era family camp, a camp consisting of old mobile homes and a recycled school bus or two scattered about, or an upscale hunting lodge where each member has their own room, they either grind their venison on-site or several people bring enough ground venison along to feed us for several days or until someone gets lucky.

We cook a great deal of ground venison meatloaf at home and we also cook a great deal of meatloaf at deer camp. The reasons may be that the preparation of meatloaf is quick and it's easy. Except for two cantankerous

ol' souls that I know, there are few members of my last camp who do not enjoy ground meat. I like meatloaf because in addition to it being served at dinner, the leftovers can also be made into sandwiches the next day—providing that there are any leftovers to enjoy.

Speaking of meatloaf sandwiches, I have a fond memory of one old retired attorney whose favorite use for leftover meatloaf at deer camp was to cut a half-inch thick slice of cold meatloaf and a half-inch slice of onion and place these between three slices of white bread and squirt on a generous portion of mustard and hot sauce. I never got close to him when he ate one of those sandwiches, but I can image that he left a pretty good trail of onion odor as he walked to his stand.

Somehow he always seemed to harvest more than his fair share of deer. Knowing what I know now about deer today and their tendency to investigate smells that they are not accustomed to, he may have been using his onion breath as a cover scent while the rest of us were spending good money for cover scents at sporting goods stores. He is probably long gone from us now, but if I am ever back in that part of the country, I will try to remember to ask him if he really liked the onion or if he knew something that he wasn't telling us.

Skillet Venison Loaf

A variation of an old Florentine recipe, this recipe calls for a food processor and few deer camps have a food processor on the counter. You may wish to bring a food processor from home or mince the cooked vegetables as small as you can.

INGREDIENTS

1 pound venison, cubed

¼ pound ham, cubed

3 eggs, lightly beaten

½ teaspoon salt

⅛ teaspoon pepper

⅛ teaspoon ground cinnamon

1 teaspoon grated lemon or lime peel

2 tablespoons all-purpose flour

2 tablespoons butter

1 medium onion, chopped fine

1 medium carrot, chopped fine

1 stalk celery, chopped fine

2 tablespoons minced parsley

1 cup canned vegetable broth, divided

1 Grind venison and ham together through fine disc 3 times.

2 To beaten eggs add salt, pepper, cinnamon and lemon peel and blend well. Gently mix in with ground meats. Lay venison mixture on a piece of aluminum foil and shape into a large loaf. Coat loaf with flour and set aside.

3 Melt butter in a skillet and sauté onion, carrot, celery and parsley about 5 minutes. Add meatloaf and brown on all sides. When meat is browned, add half of vegetable broth. Cover and simmer about 25 minutes, adding more broth if needed.

4 Place meatloaf on a hot platter and keep warm. Add remaining broth to skillet and scrape bottom of skillet. Process skillet contents in a food processor, reheat and pour some of sauce over meatloaf. Serve remaining sauce on side.

SERVES 4

Stove-Top Cheeseburger Meatloaf

INGREDIENTS

2 pounds venison burger

2 eggs

½ cup ketchup

½ cup chopped onion

2 teaspoons Worcestershire sauce

1 teaspoon prepared mustard

1 cup crushed crackers

Velveeta cheese

1 Mix all ingredients except cheese together and place in cold, heavy 10-inch skillet. Pat out, all the way to edges of skillet and cover.

2 Begin cooking on medium-high heat. After lid is too hot to touch, turn heat to lowest setting for 15 or 20 minutes. Before removing from skillet, cover top of meatloaf with slices of Velveeta cheese and replace lid just long enough for cheese to melt.

SERVES 4

Recycled Old Trailer—Deer Camp

Bourbon and Venison Loaf

INGREDIENTS

¾ cup chopped onion

¼ cup chopped green onions

½ cup chopped celery

½ cup chopped green bell pepper

4 tablespoons butter or margarine

1 tablespoon Worcestershire sauce

2 teaspoons minced garlic

2 bay leaves, halved

½ cup ketchup

2 pounds venison burger

2 eggs, lightly beaten

1 cup dry breadcrumbs

½ cup plus 2 tablespoons bourbon, divided

1 Preheat oven to 350°. Sauté onions, celery and bell pepper in butter until tender. Add Worcestershire sauce, garlic and bay leaves. Simmer until liquid evaporates. Remove from heat and remove bay leaves.

2 Combine vegetables with remaining ingredients except 2 tablespoons of bourbon and mix well. Shape into a 1½-inch high by 6-inch wide loaf and place on an ungreased cookie tray. Bake 50 to 60 minutes or until cooked through.

3 Sprinkle top of meatloaf with 2 tablespoons of bourbon before slicing and serving.

SERVES 6 TO 8

Venison Burgers

There always seems to be one or two packages of ground venison or venison burger lurking in the back of the camp freezer. If not in the camp freezer, then there are always a few packages in the freezer at someone's home. There was a time at my camp when we ran out and I mean we totally ran out of ground venison. Not one soul amongst us had even a scrap of ground venison at home and none of us knew of anyone, who was not in the woods somewhere, that would have any either.

We decided that we would make our own ground venison from the deer that were hanging in the cooler. The members voted that it was time for the camp to have its own meat grinder and that the camp should purchase the equipment. There was no debate regarding us having our own equipment and there was also no debate regarding it being purchased by the members. With all of us chipping in, the cost per person would be minimal. The debate that went on for several days was centered on whether we should purchase a manual or an electric meat grinder. Some argued that we should purchase a large electric grinding unit that would grind two whole deer an hour and could also be used to stuff the same amount of sausage. Others argued that we should purchase a small manual grinder because we would never use such a large electric unit. No one was even considering where we would purchase the equipment until the third day of debate.

Someone found a ragged copy of an old outdoor supply catalog stuffed under the couch and they drove into town to call the toll-free number to find out how long it would take to have a unit delivered to our remote location. The news wasn't good. We were well into the Christmas season and we could not be guaranteed delivery until just before the end of our hunting

season. As luck would have it, while this discussion was raging, one of the members had driven the thirty-five miles to the county seat to get a re-supply of toilet paper. While in town, he had passed a local pawnshop and had seen a small electric meat grinder that would also stuff sausage. He purchased if for himself for $79.

He should not have mentioned his little grinder when he got back to camp because it did not take long for some of that burger-hungry crew to rip that grinder from his pickup truck, saw off a hindquarter, de-bone and cube the meat.

The way those folks went after that deer and the speed at which they ran that meat through the grinder, you would have thought those folks hadn't eaten in a week. It could not have taken them more than fifteen minutes to have thirty pounds of ground venison ready for the broiler. As often happens with volunteer committee decisions, we never did purchase a grinder, we never did make any sausage at camp and, instead, we relied on our unlucky camp member to bring his little grinding machine to camp the next year.

Venison Burgers

A variation of a contemporary Belgium recipe served to the author in Mons, Belgium.

INGREDIENTS

Hamburger buns

Butter

Mustard

Tomato paste

Thin venison burger patties

Onion, sliced thin

Sliced dill pickle

1 Preheat oven to 400°. Lightly butter buns on both cut sides.

2 On 1 side spread mustard and tomato paste. On other side place raw patty. On top of patty place sliced onion and sliced pickle. Put two sides together.

3 Wrap in aluminum foil and bake about 40 minutes. Remove from oven and set aside to cool.

4 Remove foil; cut burgers into quarters.

Frozen French Canadian-Style Burgers

An old French Canadian recipe for ground venison.

INGREDIENTS

5 pounds lean venison, ground

2 pounds fat pork, ground

2 tablespoons pepper

3 tablespoons ground nutmeg

3 tablespoons salt

2 tablespoons onion powder

¼ teaspoon garlic powder

Butter or margarine or skillet drippings

1 Mix together first 7 ingredients. Shape into patties and fry in butter.

2 Wrap patties in aluminum foil or plastic wrap and freeze until ready to thaw, cook and serve.

MAKES 16 PATTIES

SAUSAGE

On occasion, I have asked myself why I make at least one quarter of each deer into sausage. I think the reason is that, like so many other hunters, I like venison sausage. For me, it could be an olfactory memory from my early youth that causes me to dedicate so much of my hard-earned deer meat to the making of several types of sausage.

One deer camp memory particularly vivid in my mind is from a long defunct deer camp of my youth. Nowhere else but at that camp have I ever seen sausage served inside of pancakes. All the activity in this camp centered around an ol' unpainted, one-story, circa 1880's clapboard-sided yeoman farmer's house and the ancient oak tree that doubled as a swing for us young folks and a place to hoist and skin deer. My dad only carried me to this camp for two years—I was probably eleven or twelve years old at the time.

As I remember the house, it had a covered porch all across the front and on the inside it had only two rooms. One was very large and wide with no interior walls, just one large room. The other room was a small kitchen that was attached to the rear that contained a full-size wood-burning cook stove and two cots.

During the off season, there was not a stitch of furniture in the house. The walls and ceiling were paneled with the original pine boards and they were covered with the peeling pages of vintage newspapers and magazines to keep the cold wind from blowing through the cracks. There was a large brick fireplace on the left wall. But since there was never a fire, I suppose that it was unsafe to use. I remember how cold it was inside that room

at night and all the hand-stitched quilts that lay strewn on the cots. For furnishings, each member brought their own cot or single bed and mattress and some probably even brought an old table and a chair or two.

The most prominent piece of furniture in the room was the battered late-night poker table that stood in the center of the room. The table's short leg rested on half of a dry goods catalog and a number of folding wooden chairs leaned up against the table.

The toilet was a privy located behind the house. I am sure this old house had no electric power, but I cannot remember how it was lit. It must have been kerosene lanterns because in those parts country folks still used them at home and most country stores still had a kerosene pump out front next to the manual gasoline pump with the glass measuring tank on top.

Back in the kitchen stood the two cots; one cot for the hired cook and one cot for the cook's helper. I wasn't much interested in watching the poker game at night or the old man that would sit on his bed and wrap the tail of his T-shirt over the mouth of a glass gallon jug to take a swig of his home brew. At my young age, these things did not interest me.

But, what did interest me was what was going on in the kitchen: watching the cook stoke the fire in the stove, smelling the burning hardwood fire, and watching as she miraculously turned out delicious meals in one large black cast-iron skillet from what seems to me like no ingredients at all.

It did not take me long to discover the kitchen was the warmest place in that cold house. I staked out my territory on the five-gallon lard can that sat against the wall on the far side of the kitchen. When we were not hunting, this was where I would spend most of my time. Often we had chicken-fried deer loin or sausage-burger patties and skillet gravy for dinner. One morning, there were several pounds of cooked venison sausage sitting on the stove that was not eaten the night before. On that particular morning, the cook directed me and the helper to break-up the cooked sausage patties while she made a pancake batter. It was from sitting on that lard can in the corner of "her" kitchen that I learned about making venison sausage pancakes.

　　　　　　　　　SAUSAGE

An Old "Wall of Missed Opportunities"

One section of the back wall was covered with dust-covered pieces of shirttails that had the previous owners name and date written on them. Since there were so few deer in this part of the country in the 1950's, the only way that we could hunt was with a shotgun and at deer that were running full speed to distance themselves from the deer dogs and outriders. Even with a shotgun you were not guaranteed a deer and a miss was more common than we were likely to admit. Deer camp rituals were as much of the experience as was the hunting.

One ritual was the cutting off of the shirttail when a deer was missed. As I remember it, the ones hanging on the wall looked like they were the whole back of the shirt. There was no way to get away from having your shirttail cut off. Since we were all standing close, out of gun range, but not out of hearing range, the standers on your right and left would hear you shoot. You either brought in a deer or you lost your shirttail to the "Wall of Missed Opportunities." The lesson soon learned was not to wear a good shirt to deer camp.

Buttermilk Pancakes
with Sausage and Hot Sorghum Butter

¼ pound venison breakfast sausage

2 cups all-purpose flour, sifted before measuring

2½ teaspoons baking powder

½ teaspoon salt

2 tablespoons sugar

1 egg, slightly beaten

1½ cups milk or buttermilk

2 tablespoons melted butter or cooking oil

Butter, cooking oil or shortening

Hot Sorghum Butter or hot syrup and butter

HOT SORGHUM BUTTER:

¾ cup sorghum molasses

½ cup butter

1 Cook venison breakfast sausage in a skillet, drain and set aside.

2 Sift together flour, baking powder, salt and sugar. Mix together egg and milk and add to flour mixture stirring only until smooth. Blend in melted butter and sausage.

3 Grease a hot griddle or large skillet. Pour in 3 tablespoons to ¼ cup of batter for each pancake. Cook until top bubbles and edges brown. Turn and cook until bottom browns.

4 Serve with Hot Sorghum Butter or hot syrup and butter.

HOT SORGHUM BUTTER:

5 Combine molasses and butter in a small saucepan and heat until butter is melted. Serve hot. Makes about 1 cup.

SERVES 4

Scotch Eggs

1 pound Fried Spiced-Garlic Venison Sausage (page 96) or other bulk sausage

4 hard-boiled eggs

1 cup unseasoned breadcrumbs

Shortening or oil for deep-frying

4 slices toasted thick-cut bread

Prepared honey-mustard sauce

1 Divide sausage into 4 equal portions and roll out each to ½-inch thickness.

2 Lay a hard-boiled egg on an outside edge and roll egg to cover with sausage. Press sausage to cover all egg.

3 Roll in unseasoned breadcrumbs and deep-fry until sausage is done. Remove and allow to drain and cool.

4 Slice sausage egg into ½-inch-thick slices, place on toasted thick-cut bread and serve with honey-mustard sauce.

SERVES 4

SAUSAGE

Fried Spiced-Garlic Sausage

INGREDIENTS

2 pounds boneless venison, minced

¾ pound pork fat, minced

1 small white onion, minced

4 large cloves garlic, minced

2 teaspoons salt

1 teaspoon black pepper

1 teaspoon ground sage

½ teaspoon ground thyme

¼ teaspoon ground nutmeg

¼ teaspoon ground ginger

⅛ teaspoon ground allspice

1 Mix all ingredients and grind once with a course grinding disc. Grind again with a fine grinding disc and make into patties.

2 Cook to 160° or package and freeze.

SERVES 8

Fried Venison Link Sausage

This method of cooking sausage was brought to America by early German immigrants. The sausage will shrink very little and will be moist inside.

INGREDIENTS

Link venison sausage

Water

Real butter

1 Place sausage in a frying pan and just barely cover with water. Cover and boil 5 to 10 minutes. Remove sausage and wipe skillet clean.

2 To skillet, add a small amount of butter and melt over medium heat. Return sausage to pan and cook over medium heat until skins are just brown, turning frequently.

Sweet Sausage Butter Biscuits

This is way that my grandmother made her biscuits when I was a young boy. With lard and real butter, this is not what we would call a very "healthy" meal today. However, if you are willing to take a once-in-a-year chance, this recipe will give you a true taste of real old-fashioned country sausage and biscuit. My preferred way of enjoying these biscuits is to eat them in my tree stand along with a thermos of hot chocolate. Don't you worry about smell spooking your deer. Over the years, I have harvested just as many deer after eating these biscuits as I have without them.

INGREDIENTS

- 2 to 2½ cups self-rising flour plus more for dusting
- ½ cup lard or shortening
- 1 cup buttermilk
- Real butter, softened
- Sorghum or other dark molasses
- 8 to 10 cooked venison sausage patties
- Salt and pepper to taste

1 Heat oven to 475°. Grease a baking sheet.

2 Place flour in large bowl and make a crater in center. Add lard and buttermilk; work mixture with your fingers just until dough is soft and sticky. Place on floured surface and sift a little flour on top. Gently knead just until dough is no longer sticky.

3 Roll dough to ¾ inch thick. Cut with a biscuit cutter; do not twist. Place biscuits, with edges touching, on baking sheet. Bake 8 minutes or until tops are brown.

4 Open biscuits and place a pat of butter inside. Close and allow butter to melt. Reopen biscuit, spoon on molasses, lay on sausage patty and season with salt and pepper.

5 Wrap each biscuit in aluminum foil and stick them in your hunting bag.

MAKES 8 TO 10 BISCUITS

Breakfast Venison Egg Squares

1 (16-ounce) loaf Pepperidge Farm bread

2 pounds venison breakfast sausage

¾ pound Cheddar cheese, shredded

8 eggs, beaten

4 cups half-and-half

2 tablespoons Worcestershire sauce

1 teaspoon dry mustard

1 teaspoon salt

½ teaspoon pepper

1 Remove crust from bread and cut into cubes.

2 Brown venison sausage in a skillet and drain. Place sausage on bottom of a 9x13-inch casserole dish. Place bread on top of sausage and cover with cheese.

3 Whisk remaining ingredients and pour over cheese. Cover and bake 45 to 50 minutes.

4 Cut into squares and serve.

SERVES 4 TO 6

Cream-Style Corn, Egg and Sausage Casserole

INGREDIENTS

4 eggs, beaten

2½ cups canned cream-style corn

1 cup packed soft breadcrumbs

1 pound venison breakfast sausage, cooked

1 teaspoon salt

½ teaspoon pepper

6 tablespoons ketchup

1 Preheat oven to 350°. Mix all ingredients except ketchup.

2 Pour mixture into an ovenproof casserole dish and spoon ketchup over top. Bake 50 to 60 minutes.

SERVES 6

*Cream-Style Corn, Egg and
Sausage Casserole*

Lasagna with Venison Sausage

VENISON TOMATO SAUCE:

4 tablespoons olive oil

½ pound spicy link Italian venison sausage or other link sausage, chopped

2 teaspoons minced fresh basil

2 cloves garlic, chopped

Pinch salt

Pinch pepper

1 (6-ounce) can tomato paste

1 (28-ounce) can crushed Italian tomatoes

LASAGNA:

¾ pound fresh mushrooms, sliced

Lemon juice

Olive oil

1 pound dry lasagna noodles

2 cups crumbled ricotta cheese

1½ cups shredded mozzarella cheese

Romano cheese, grated

VENISON TOMATO SAUCE:

1 Heating olive oil in a saucepan. Add sausage, basil, garlic, salt and pepper. Sauté mixture 3 to 4 minutes and then add tomato paste and crushed tomatoes. Simmer until sauce is thick; set aside.

LASAGNA:

2 Cook sliced mushrooms in a small amount of water with a little lemon juice and olive oil until soft; set aside.

3 Boil lasagna noodles in salted water until soft; place on damp towels to drain. Place a layer of noodles on bottom of an oiled baking dish.

4 Mix ricotta and mozzarella cheeses. Add a layer of cheese, a layer of mushrooms and a layer of Venison Tomato Sauce. Continue alternating layers ending with a layer of sauce. Add a final layer of Romano cheese.

5 Bake in a preheated 425° oven 15 minutes.

SERVES 4 TO 6

Baked Zucchini Squash, Cheese and Sausage

INGREDIENTS

½ pound venison breakfast sausage, cooked and drained

2 pounds zucchini, sliced

1 cup Bisquick mix

½ cup butter, melted

3 eggs, beaten

1 cup shredded Cheddar cheese, divided

Salt and pepper to taste

1 Preheat oven to 350°. Butter a 2-quart ovenproof casserole dish.

2 Mix sausage, zucchini, Bisquick, butter and eggs together with ½ cup Cheddar cheese. Season with a small amount of salt and pepper.

3 Pour into casserole dish, top with remaining ½ cup Cheddar cheese and bake 1 hour.

SERVES 4

Yellow Squash and Sausage

INGREDIENTS

1 pound venison sausage

1 large onion, chopped coarse

4 cups sliced yellow squash

2 tablespoons butter, melted

1 cup shredded Cheddar cheese

1 cup cracker crumbs

4 eggs, beaten

1 Preheat oven to 350°. Crumble sausage and cook with onion until sausage is done and onions are clear; set aside.

2 Sauté squash in butter until fork-tender.

3 Mix together sausage, squash, melted butter, cheese and cracker crumbs.

4 Fold in beaten eggs and bake in greased 3-quart casserole dish for 40 minutes.

SERVES 4

Slow Cooker Sausage and Red Beans

INGREDIENTS

1 pound dried dark red kidney beans

Hot water

1½ pounds link venison sausage

1 white or yellow onion, diced

1 tablespoon garlic salt

1 teaspoon pepper

Hot sauce to taste

3 cups cooked white rice

1 Place beans in slow cooker; add water to cover by 2 inches. Cook on high 1 hour.

2 Slice sausage into ¼- to ½-inch-thick pieces. Add sausage, onion, garlic salt and pepper to slow cooker. Cook another 4 hours or until beans are tender.

3 Season with hot sauce to taste. Serve over rice.

SERVES 6

Baked Rice and Sausage

INGREDIENTS

1 pound venison breakfast sausage

1 white or yellow onion, chopped

1 cup chopped green bell pepper

1 cup raw rice

1 cup chopped celery

2 (10.75-ounce) cans cream of chicken soup

1½ soup cans water

1 Preheat oven to 350°. Fry sausage, drain and crumble. Place sausage in bottom of an ovenproof 3-quart casserole dish.

2 Mix remaining ingredients and pour over sausage. Bake 45 to 60 minutes.

SERVES 4

Apple, Cranberry & Sausage Stuffing

Shortening or vegetable oil

10 cups cubed day-old sourdough bread

1½ pounds venison breakfast sausage

2 tablespoons butter or margarine

2 cups diced celery

2 cups diced onions

Salt and pepper to taste

2 apples, peeled, cored and diced

1½ cups dried cranberries

¼ cup chopped fresh sage

1 cup chopped fresh parsley

2 tablespoons chopped fresh rosemary

1 tablespoon chopped fresh thyme

1 cup chopped toasted walnuts

2 eggs

½ cup butter, melted

2 cups chicken or beef broth

SERVES 6 TO 8

1 Preheat oven to 350°. Grease a 9x13-inch ovenproof baking dish or disposable aluminum baking pan.

2 Spread bread cubes in a thin layer onto 2 or more baking sheets. Bake in oven until bread cubes have toasted evenly, 5 to 7 minutes. Stir once. Place toasted bread cubes into a very large mixing bowl and set aside.

3 Heat a large skillet, add sausage, break up and fry until brown. Drain sausage and add to bread cubes.

4 Add 2 tablespoons butter to skillet and melt. Stir in celery and onions and sauté until onions turn clear. Season with salt and pepper. Add vegetables to bread cubes. Stir in apples, cranberries, sage, parsley, rosemary, thyme and walnuts.

5 Whisk eggs and melted butter into chicken broth and pour over bread cubes. Gently stir egg and broth mixture into bread cubes until liquid has been absorbed.

6 Pack stuffing into baking dish, cover with aluminum foil and bake 30 minutes. Remove aluminum foil, stir and bake another 15 minutes or until top is brown.

Baked Macaroni, Cheese and Sausage

INGREDIENTS

- 1 cup uncooked elbow macaroni
- ½ teaspoon caraway seed
- ½ teaspoon dry mustard
- ½ cup chopped onion
- ¼ pound Velveeta cheese, cubed
- ¾ cup milk
- 1 pound link venison sausage, sliced ½ inch thick
- ¼ teaspoon paprika

1 Preheat oven to 350°. Grease a 2-quart ovenproof casserole dish.

2 Cook macaroni according to package directions and drain.

3 Mix in caraway seed and mustard. Place half of macaroni in greased casserole. Top with half the onion and half the cheese. Layer remaining macaroni, onion and cheese.

4 Pour over with milk. Cover and bake 45 minutes.

5 While baking, fry venison sausage in a skillet.

6 After 45 minutes, remove casserole, lay on venison sausage slices, sprinkle with paprika and bake another 15 minutes.

SERVES 4

Baked Spicy Potato and Sausage

INGREDIENTS

1½ cups thin-sliced potatoes

¾ pound spicy link venison sausage, cut in small pieces

½ cup chopped onion

½ cup chopped green bell peppers

6 eggs

½ cup milk

½ teaspoon hot sauce

¾ teaspoon baking powder

¼ cup grated Parmesan cheese

½ cup canned tomato sauce

4 ounces shredded mozzarella cheese

1 Preheat oven to 375°. Grease a 2–quart ovenproof casserole dish.

2 Layer dish with potatoes, sausage, onion and pepper and bake 35 to 40 minutes. Remove from oven and reduce oven to 325°.

3 Beat together eggs, milk, hot sauce, baking powder and Parmesan cheese and pour over sausage. Bake 30 minutes.

4 Spoon tomato sauce on top, lay on mozzarella cheese and bake another 10 minutes.

SERVES 4 TO 6

Quick Venison Patty and Sweet Potato Casserole

INGREDIENTS

6 baked sweet potatoes

¼ cup sugar

Juice and zest of 1 lemon

1 teaspoon cinnamon

1 pound venison sausage
patties, cooked

1 Preheat oven to 450°. Mix together pulp from sweet potatoes, sugar, lemon juice, lemon zest and cinnamon. Beat until light or mix in a food processor.

2 Butter an ovenproof casserole dish and pour in sweet potato mixture. Cover with sausage patties and bake 10 minutes.

SERVES 4 TO 6

Baked Link Sausage and Sweet Potatoes

INGREDIENTS

1 pound venison link sausage,
cooked and drained

3 cups cooked and mashed
sweet potatoes

1 cup applesauce

2 eggs, beaten

½ teaspoon salt

½ teaspoon cinnamon

¼ teaspoon nutmeg

1 Preheat oven to 350°. Slice cooked sausage and set aside.

2 Into sweet potatoes, mix in applesauce, eggs, salt, cinnamon and nutmeg.

3 Pour sweet potato mixture into an ovenproof baking dish. Arrange venison slices on top and bake 25 to 30 minutes.

SERVES 4 TO 6

Lima Beans and Smoked Sausage

INGREDIENTS

4 cups fresh or frozen lima beans

2 tablespoons bacon drippings

¾ cup finely chopped onion

2 cups smoked venison link sausage, sliced ¼ inch thick

1 teaspoon salt

½ teaspoon black pepper

1 Put beans in 3-quart pot and just cover with water. Bring to a boil and cook until just tender.

2 While beans are cooking, put bacon drippings, onion and venison sausage in skillet and cook until light brown.

3 When beans are tender, add sausage, onion, salt and pepper to boiling beans. Cover and cook on medium heat 10 minutes.

SERVES 4 TO 6

Baked Broccoli and Sausage

INGREDIENTS

1 pound venison breakfast sausage, cooked

2 (14-ounce) packages frozen broccoli, cooked and well drained

2 eggs, beaten

1 cup breadcrumbs

½ cup mayonnaise

½ tablespoon prepared mustard

¼ cup sliced water chestnuts

1 Preheat oven to 350°. Grease an 8x12-inch ovenproof baking dish or disposable aluminum baking pan.

2 Mix sausage, broccoli, eggs and breadcrumbs and pour into pan. Bake 30 minutes.

3 During last 5 minutes, spread with mayonnaise and mustard and top with water chestnuts.

SERVES 4 TO 6

Spicy Jalapeño Bread
with Sausage

To make non-spicy bread, omit jalapeño pepper and hot pepper sauce.

INGREDIENTS

- 1 pound venison breakfast sausage
- 1 small onion, chopped
- 1 jalapeño, finely chopped
- 2 cups buttermilk baking mix
- ¼ cup butter or margarine, melted
- 1 teaspoon salt
- 2 teaspoons chopped fresh parsley
- ½ cup shredded Swiss cheese
- ¼ cup grated Parmesan cheese
- 1 egg, beaten
- ¼ teaspoon hot pepper sauce
- ⅓ cup milk

1 Preheat oven to 400°. Grease a 9x13-inch baking pan or disposable aluminum baking pan.

2 Break up sausage in a skillet; mix in onion and jalapeño. Brown mixture, drain and set aside to cool.

3 Mix together biscuit mix, butter, salt and parsley.

4 Mix together cheeses, egg, hot sauce and milk; stir into biscuit mixture. Add biscuit-cheese to sausage mixture and stir well.

5 Pour bread mix into greased pan and bake 35 minutes or until a toothpick inserted into center comes out clean.

SERVES 6

ROAST

Meat Thermometers

The biggest mistake that most of us make when cooking a venison roast is that we over-cook it until it has the consistency of harness leather. Since venison and other wild game and fowl have virtually no fat in their muscles, they do not cook like a beef roast. Unlike beef, where the internal temperature slowly progresses through raw, medium rare, medium, medium well, and well done, venison passes though raw, medium rare, medium, and then it goes straight up and past well done in a moment. With venison, some compare eating an over-cooked venison roast with trying to eat dry rubber.

Forget all that you have ever heard about cooking a venison roast based on its weight versus oven temperature versus time. That method of cooking absolutely does not work with a venison roast.

What does work, and works very well, is an ovenproof internal meat thermometer. Only an internal meat thermometer will tell you exactly when your roast is at the proper internal temperature and that

111

internal temperature is 138° to 140° and absolutely no more. When the internal temperature of your venison roast reaches 138° to 140°, immediately remove it from the oven, leave the thermometer in the roast, wrap the roast in aluminum foil and allow it to rest 10 to 15 minutes before slicing.

You will notice that your thermometer will continue to rise to around 148° to 150°—which is perfect and where you want it to be. At this temperature, the inside of the roast is cooked to medium. If you keep your roast in the oven until the internal temperature reaches 148° to 150°, when you remove the roast the temperature will continue to rise to past 160°. At this internal temperature, your roast will be as dry as wallpaper. By wrapping your roast in aluminum foil and allowing it to rest before slicing, the juices stay inside, cease moving around, and the roast remains moist.

If you are cooking for a large group of hunters, a large oven-cooked roast, such as Buttermilk and Spice Marinated Roast (page 115), may be the easiest and quickest thing to cook. However, if you are only cooking for four to six hunters, you may want to cook one of the smaller roasts such as Bacon and Vegetable Stuffed and Rolled Venison Round Steak Roast (page 116) or Roasted Venison & Vegetables (page 114).

Oven-Baked Loin
with Blackberry Sauce

This recipe calls for a sieve or hand-turned food mill and few deer camps have these items in the pot drawer. However, they are very inexpensive and can be purchased at any chain discount store. I would recommend a food mill as it is much easier to use.

INGREDIENTS

1 (12-inch long) piece of venison loin, cut from large end

Cotton twine

Cooking oil

BLACKBERRY SAUCE:

½ cup blackberries or raspberries, fresh or frozen

¼ cup rice wine vinegar

2 tablespoons dark brown sugar

¼ teaspoon ground cinnamon

⅛ teaspoon ground nutmeg

⅛ teaspoon ground cloves

⅛ teaspoon cayenne pepper

¼ teaspoon salt

1 Preheat oven to 350°. Tie loin tightly every 1 to 1½ inches with cotton twine. Rub tied loin with cooking oil; insert a meat thermometer deep into small end of tied loin. Bake until internal temperature reaches 138°.

2 Remove loin from oven. Wrap with aluminum foil and allow to rest 10 to 15 minutes.

3 Remove string and slice in ½-inch-thick pieces.

4 Drizzle Blackberry Sauce onto serving plates and place 2 slices on top of sauce.

BLACKBERRY SAUCE:

5 Rub blackberries through a fine sieve or hand-turned food mill.

6 In a small saucepan, combine blackberry juice and remaining ingredients and heat until slightly thickened.

SERVES 6

Basic Baked Venison Roast

INGREDIENTS

1 (3-pound) boneless venison roast

Cotton twine

2 onions, quartered and separated

3 teaspoons garlic powder

1 teaspoon salt

1 teaspoon pepper

1 Preheat oven to 300°. Tie roast with cotton twine.

2 Make cuts into roast and insert a sliver of onion into each cut. Sprinkle with garlic powder, salt and pepper.

3 Wrap and seal roast in foil.

4 Add water to bottom of a roasting pan. Add a rack and place roast on rack. Bake until internal thermometer reaches 138° to 140° (1½ to 2 hours).

5 Allow to rest 10 minutes. Unwrap and save juices for gravy.

SERVES 4

Roasted Venison & Vegetables

INGREDIENTS

1 (4-pound) venison roast, deboned

1 (1-ounce) envelope dehydrated vegetable soup mix, divided

Cotton twine

Rosemary sprigs

Assorted cooked spring vegetables

1 Preheat oven to 350°. Coat roast with soup mix and wrap and seal roast in foil. Tie with cotton twine.

2 Roast until internal temperature reaches 138° to 140°. Rest before removing foil.

3 Slice and garnish with rosemary sprigs and serve with spring vegetables.

SERVES 6

Buttermilk and Spice Marinated Roast

INGREDIENTS

1 deboned and rolled venison hindquarter roast

Cotton twine

1 head garlic, cloves cut into slivers plus 6 cloves garlic, chopped fine, divided

1 tablespoon black pepper

2 teaspoons cayenne pepper

1 teaspoon ground thyme

1 teaspoon ground sage

1 tablespoon apple cider vinegar

1 pound thick-cut smoked bacon

4 onions, chopped

4 bay leaves, halved

1 teaspoon whole black peppercorns

1 (3- to 4-inch) cinnamon stick, halved

½ gallon buttermilk

4 tablespoons cooking oil

2 cans or more beer, divided

3 large onions, quartered

3 carrots, peeled and halved

2 sweet potatoes, peeled and halved

3 tart apples, peeled, cored and quartered

1 Tie rolled roast with cotton twine. Every inch or so, insert tip of a knife into the meat and insert a sliver of garlic.

2 Mix together black pepper, cayenne pepper, thyme, sage and vinegar and rub into roast. Lay strips of bacon on top. Wrap roast in aluminum foil and let rest 6 hours in the refrigerator.

3 Mix together onions, bay leaves, chopped garlic, peppercorns, cinnamon and buttermilk. Place venison in marinade and refrigerate 48 hours. Turn roast several times each day. Drain roast and discard marinade.

4 Preheat oven to 300°. Brown roast well in oil in a large heavy pot or Dutch oven. Drain grease. Pour in 1 beer. Cover and bake 1 to 2 hours or until internal temperature reaches 125°.

5 Add vegetables and apples and remaining beer. Continue to cook until vegetables and roast are tender and internal temperature of roast reaches 138° to 140°.

SERVES 10+

Bacon and Vegetable Stuffed and Rolled Round Steak Roast

9 slices bacon, divided

1 medium onion, chopped

½ cup chopped celery

½ cup chopped carrot

⅓ cup seasoned dry breadcrumbs

2 teaspoons dried parsley flakes

¼ teaspoon salt

⅛ teaspoon pepper

3 to 4 pounds venison top round steak roast, cut 1 inch thick

Cotton twine

1 Preheat oven to 325°. Fry 6 bacon slices in large skillet over medium heat until crisp. Remove from heat. Transfer bacon to paper towels to drain. Reserve 3 tablespoons bacon fat in skillet.

2 Crumble drained bacon and set aside.

3 Cook and stir onion, celery and carrot in reserved bacon fat over medium heat until tender. Remove from heat. Stir in crumbled bacon, breadcrumbs, parsley flakes, salt and pepper.

4 Spread vegetable mixture evenly on roast, patting it firmly into place. Roll up jelly-roll style and tie in several places with cotton twine. Place rolled roast in roasting pan. Top roast with remaining 3 slices uncooked bacon. Roast until internal thermometer registers 138° to 140°.

5 Remove roast, cover and allow to rest 10 minutes. Slice and serve.

SERVES 4 TO 6

Bone-In Leg Roast Supreme

1 bone-in whole venison hindquarter

Salt and pepper to taste

10 juniper berries

5 cloves garlic, crushed

5 sprigs fresh rosemary, minced

¼ cup lemon juice

½ cup water

1 cup dry white wine

1 Preheat oven to 450°. Remove visible fat from venison leg and make 5 long cuts on top. Season roast and cuts with salt and pepper.

2 Crush juniper berries and mix with crushed garlic and rosemary. Spoon mixture into the cuts.

3 Place venison on a roasting rack in a baking pan and pour over with lemon juice. Add water into bottom of pan. Place in oven and bake 20 minutes.

4 Reduce heat to 350° and continue to roast until the internal temperature reaches 138° to 140°. Baste occasionally with pan juices during cooking. Remove roast, cover and allow to rest 10 minutes.

5 Remove roasting rack from pan and spoon off excess fat from remaining juices. Add wine and stir well to mix with pan juices. Boil 5 to 10 minutes to reduce.

6 Slice and serve venison with the sauce.

SERVES 10 TO 12

Potato and Carrot Slow Cooker Roast

2-inch-thick venison round roast or large chunks

2 large chunks beef fat

3 medium onions, whole, halved, sliced or chopped

8 small potatoes, whole, halved or quartered

2 medium carrots, halved, quartered or sliced

1 garlic clove, whole, sliced or chopped

1¾ to 2 cups French onion soup

Salt and pepper to taste

1 Place roast, beef fat, onions, potatoes, carrots and garlic in a crockpot. Pour in soup and season to taste with salt and pepper.

2 Set crockpot on low and cook 8 hours.

SERVES 4 TO 6

Simple Bacon and Venison Slow-Cooked Roast

1 (3-pound) venison roast

½ cup water

2 beef bouillon cubes

1 pound sliced smoked bacon

1 Place venison roast in a slow cooker. Pour in water and crumble bouillon cubes over roast.

2 Lay strips of bacon on top of roast. Turn slow cooker on low, cover and cook 8 hours.

SERVES 4

Pot Roast with Mushrooms and Onion Soup Mix

½ cup all-purpose flour

Pepper to taste

1 (4-to 5-pound) venison roast

¼ cup vegetable oil

1 (10.75-ounce) can cream of mushroom soup

1 soup can water

1 (1-ounce) package dry onion soup mix

1 Season flour with pepper. Rub mixture into roast.

2 Heat oil in a large pot and brown roast on all sides. Mix mushroom soup, water and onion soup mix. Pour over roast.

3 Cover and cook over very low heat 2 to 3 hours or until a meat thermometer registers 140°. Turn meat occasionally and add more water if necessary.

SERVES 6 TO 10

Basque-Style Slow Cooked Roast

1 (3-pound) venison roast

3 garlic cloves, sliced

Salt and pepper to taste

1 large onion, sliced

1 large green bell pepper, sliced

1 (4-ounce) jar whole pimento

3 slices smoked bacon, quartered

1 Pierce venison and insert pieces of garlic. Place roast in a slow cooker. Season with salt and pepper.

2 Cover roast with onion, bell pepper, pimento and bacon. Add small amount of water.

3 Cover and cook on low 6 to 8 hours, basting occasionally.

SERVES 4

ROAST

Stove-Top Spicy Italian Roast

INGREDIENTS

1 (5-pound) venison roast

1½ cups water

1½ teaspoons salt

1½ teaspoons dried oregano

6 cloves garlic, crushed

1½ teaspoons red pepper flakes, optional

2 bay leaves, halved

½ teaspoon garlic powder

2 teaspoons dried basil

1 Place roast in large pot or Dutch oven.

2 Combine water and remaining ingredients and stir well. Pour over roast and bring to boil.

3 Cover, reduce heat, and simmer 3 to 4 hours or until tender. Remove from stove and allow to cool. Cover and chill in refrigerator.

4 Remove roast and cut into very thin slices. Return to broth; cook over medium heat until thoroughly heated. Remove bay leaves before serving.

SERVES 12

Pot Roast with Salt Pork

INGREDIENTS

1 (4- to 5-pound) venison roast

Salt and pepper to taste

6 slices salt pork, ⅛ inch thin

2 lemons, 1 juiced, 1 sliced thin, divided

2 tablespoons Worcestershire sauce

1 medium onion, chopped

1 Preheat oven to 350°. Season roast with salt and pepper.

2 Wash excess salt from salt pork and use it to line the inside of a roasting pan. Add lemon juice, Worcestershire sauce, onion and lemon slices. Insert a meat thermometer into thickest part of roast and cook until internal temperature reaches 140°. Add additional water if needed.

SERVES 8 TO 10

Marinated Stove-Top Creole-Flavored Roast

INGREDIENTS

8 ounces Italian salad dressing

8 ounces water

2 cloves garlic, minced

⅛ teaspoon red pepper

⅛ teaspoon black pepper

¼ teaspoon hot sauce

¼ teaspoon salt

3 tablespoons minced fresh thyme

3 tablespoons minced fresh rosemary

3 tablespoons minced fresh basil

1 (5-pound) rolled venison sirloin roast

1 cup olive oil, divided

1 cup all-purpose flour

2 onions, diced

1 bell pepper, diced

2 cups chopped celery

Filé powder, optional

1 Make marinade by mixing salad dressing and water.

2 Mix together garlic, red and black peppers, hot sauce, salt, thyme, rosemary and basil.

3 Make many small and deep cuts into roast and stuff with spice mixture. Cover and marinate in refrigerator 24 hours.

4 Brown venison roast in a large pot or Dutch oven with ½ cup olive oil. Remove roast and set aside.

5 Add remaining ½ cup olive oil and flour to the pot. Make a roux by very gently browning the flour; stir constantly. Be careful not to burn the flour. If flour burns, start over again.

6 To the roux, add onions, bell pepper, and celery and cook until vegetables are limp. Return roast to pot, cover with water and simmer about 5 hours until the venison is tender.

7 Offer filé powder on the table for those that would like to thicken their gravy.

SERVES 4

ROAST

Green Onion, Venison and Cheese Omelet

A great way to use that leftover roast.

½ cup chopped green onions

2 tablespoons butter, divided

½ cup chopped cooked cold venison roast

6 eggs

2 tablespoons milk

¼ cup diced Cheddar cheese

1 tablespoon chopped pimento

Salt and pepper to taste

1 Sauté onions in 1 tablespoon butter until just clear. Mix in venison to warm it up and set aside.

2 Whisk eggs with milk and fry in remaining 1 tablespoon butter until beginning to firm on bottom.

3 Top with onion-venison mixture, cheese and pimento. Season with salt and pepper to taste.

4 Fold omelet over, remove omelet from pan and cut in half.

SERVES 2

VARIETY MEATS

An Acquired Taste

I have a number of good friends that enjoy these "special" cuts of venison, just as they enjoy the equivalent "special" cuts of meat from beeves and swine. I do not eat very many specialty meats from my deer. I am of the opinion that these meats are an acquired taste, and to enjoy these meats, that taste must be acquired early in life.

My father enjoyed an occasional cow's brain and scrambled eggs for breakfast and when we had squirrel stew for dinner, he was known to chomp down on a squirrel head. My father was born in 1915 and his formative years were lived during the Great Depression in a rural land-poor area of the Deep South. It was a time when the game that one harvested or did not harvest that day was what the family ate or did not eat that night for dinner. My dad once told me that when he was in his early teens that his Uncle Jake would give him one shotgun shell and send him off to the woods. Those were tough times and every edible bit of the animal ended up on the table in one fashion or another.

My formative years were the late 1940's and early 1950's. For many of us growing up the United States, this was a prosperous period and my mom shopped at the supermarket. I had few occasions to come into contact with variety meats. With the exception of fried pork cracklings (skins) found in today's convenience stores and the occasional pickled pigs' feet and eggs

Miss Anne Visiting a Red Deer Farm in Scotland

found in rural gas stations, I do not have occasion to eat variety meats.

However, I do enjoy braised venison shank. For years, I threw these parts of my deer away under the assumption that there was very little edible meat on those leg bones, and what meat was there was tough and stringy. In 1996, I made a trip to Europe and I often saw shanks on the menu. I asked my Scottish friends about this and they informed me that in Europe, braised (slow simmering in a liquid) shanks were a delicacy, tender and quite tasty. I questioned this. One night, they made Osso Buco and it was delicious. As it was explained to me, shanks have a great deal of collagen (tough white sinew tissue). However, when braised, the collagen breaks down and the meat becomes very tender. The trick is to cut the shank into 2-inch-long sections and stand them on end in the braising liquid. What was served to me was so good that I developed a recipe of my own and entered it in an international cooking contest.

International Cooking Contest Winners—
Antinori Estates in Tuscany

This contest was co-sponsored by *Saveur* magazine and Antinori Winery. I was lucky to have my recipe for Venison Osso Buco chosen as one of the five international winners. The prize was a two-week cooking tour for two, visiting and staying at a number of the Antinori vineyards and estates located in the Tuscan region of Italy and included the opportunity to cook with and learn from the estate chefs. Not a bad deal for an ol' southern country boy.

If you have members of your camp who enjoy these special cuts of meat, I think they will find a recipe here they will enjoy. If you are not one of this select group, I suggest you try one of the Osso Buco recipes. You will be surprised at how delicious it is and you may never throw a deer shank away again.

Braised Venison Shanks
in White Wine Sauce

INGREDIENTS

8 pieces venison shank, cut 1½ to 2 inches long

¼ cup olive oil

⅓ cup butter

Salt and pepper to taste

2 to 3 cups inexpensive dry white wine

1 lemon

8 tablespoons minced fresh parsley

1 Dredge venison shanks in flour. In a large, deep skillet, heat olive oil and butter over medium heat until butter stops foaming. Add venison shanks and arrange in a single layer. Cook over moderately high heat until brown on 1 side. Sprinkle with salt and pepper.

2 Turn meat, brown other side and season with salt and pepper. Add enough wine to almost cover meat. Reduce heat to a low simmer. Cover and simmer 2½ hours.

3 Remove venison shanks to a warm plate and cover with foil.

4 Peel a thin layer of rind from the lemon and cut into long, fine strips. Add lemon peel and chopped parsley to sauce and boil several minutes to slightly reduce. Stir bottom to loosen any brown bits and whisk frequently to prevent burning.

5 Remove from heat and carefully return venison shanks to the pot. Cover and allow shanks to reheat.

SERVES 4

Baked Osso Buco
with Beer and Mustard Sauce

INGREDIENTS

1½ (12-ounce) bottles dark beer

16 ounces canned beef broth

2 ounces tomato paste

½ teaspoon cinnamon

½ teaspoon English or French mustard

1 teaspoon ground red pepper

1 teaspoon cumin

⅛ cup packed dark brown sugar

4 venison shanks, cut 2 inches long

1 Preheat oven to 300°. Mix together all ingredients except venison.

2 Place shanks in a small ovenproof pan or high-sided casserole dish standing on end. Pour in beer mixture. Add water to cover if needed. Bring to a boil, skim off foam, cover and bake 2 hours.

SERVES 6

Crusted Venison Liver
in Lemon-Butter Sauce

INGREDIENTS

1 pound venison liver

Salt and pepper to taste

All-purpose flour

1 egg, slightly beaten

Cracker crumbs

4 tablespoons butter, divided

1 tablespoon olive oil

2 tablespoons lemon juice

½ teaspoon sugar

1 Clean venison liver and cut crosswise into ½-inch-thick slices. Sprinkle with salt and pepper and dredge with flour. Dip into beaten egg and roll in cracker crumbs.

2 Melt 2 tablespoons butter in a skillet; add olive oil and cook liver slices until brown on outside and dark on the inside.

3 While liver is cooking, melt remaining butter in another pan and stir in lemon juice and sugar. Stir until sugar is dissolved.

4 When liver is done, remove to a serving platter and pour lemon-butter sauce over liver.

SERVES 2 TO 4

Fried Venison Liver
with Hot Mustard Sauce

This recipe calls for a double boiler and few deer camps have a double boiler in the pot drawer. However, these pots are very inexpensive and can be purchased at any chain discount store.

INGREDIENTS

5 teaspoons dry mustard

½ cup more or less water

1 pound venison liver

1 cup all-purpose flour

1 teaspoon salt

½ teaspoon pepper

2 teaspoons nutmeg

Vegetable oil

3 eggs, lightly beaten

¾ cup sugar

¾ cup apple cider vinegar

Ketchup

Parsley sprigs

Shaved fresh ginger

1 Mix dry mustard with water until it is the consistency of heavy cream. Set aside in refrigerator 2 hours.

2 Clean liver and cut off all connective tissue. Cut into 1-inch pieces and wash in cold water. Allow to drain.

3 Season flour with salt, pepper and nutmeg. Dredge liver in flour mixture, a few pieces at a time. Heat ¼ inch of vegetable oil in a skillet and fry liver until crust is crisp.

4 Place eggs, sugar and vinegar in a blender and process until smooth. Cook egg mixture in a double boiler until vinegar taste is gone. Remove mixture from stove and add just enough ketchup to change the color from yellow to light orange.

5 After mixture has cooled, add chilled mustard mixture to taste.

6 Spoon sauce onto individual serving plates and lay venison liver on top. Garnish with parsley and shaved ginger.

SERVES 4

Venison Mountain Oysters
with Fried Parsley and Spicy Tomato Sauce

INGREDIENTS

4 venison testicles

¼ cup olive oil

2 tablespoons lemon juice

1 teaspoon chopped tarragon leaves

1 cup large sprigs of curly parsley

1 cup plus 2 teaspoons lard or vegetable oil, divided

1 egg, lightly beaten

3 tablespoons whole milk

¾ cup sifted unseasoned breadcrumbs

All-purpose flour

Salt and pepper to taste

¼ cup butter, softened

Tomato sauce

Tabasco sauce

Worcestershire sauce

SERVES 8 (20-YEAR-OLDS) OR 1 (50-YEAR-OLD)

1. Remove loose outer skin from venison and very carefully remove inner skin. Cover with cold water; refrigerate 3 hours. Change cold water each hour.

2. Place venison in a pot, cover with cold water and bring to a boil. Reduce heat and simmer 5 minutes. Drain and cover with ice water and let stand until cold.

3. Combine olive oil, lemon juice and tarragon. Slice venison ¼ inch thick and marinate in mixture 1 to 2 hours.

4. Deep-fry parsley sprigs in 1 cup lard until wilted. Set aside to drain.

5. In a bowl, mix egg, milk and remaining 2 teaspoons lard. Place breadcrumbs in a second bowl. In a third bowl, combine flour with salt and pepper to taste.

6. Drain venison slices and dry thoroughly. Dredge each slice in seasoned flour; shake to remove excess. Coat in egg mixture, then cover with breadcrumbs. Place on a wire rack to dry 15 minutes.

7. Melt butter in a heated skillet. Sauté slices on all sides until golden brown.

8. Serve with tomato sauce seasoned to taste with Tabasco and Worcestershire. Garnish with fried parsley.

VARIETY MEATS

Traditional Scottish Haggis

Haggis is traditionally served as "Haggis, Neeps and Tatties." The Neeps are mashed turnips with a little milk and allspice added. Tatties are creamed potatoes, flavored with a little nutmeg.

INGREDIENTS

1 deer or sheep's stomach, washed

Salt

1 venison heart

1 venison liver

¾ cup rolled oats

½ pound beef suet, chopped fine

3 onions, chopped fine

1 teaspoon salt

½ teaspoon pepper

¼ teaspoon red pepper

½ teaspoon nutmeg

¾ cup canned beef broth

Cotton twine

Neeps for 8 to 12

Tatties for 8 to 12

1 Wash stomach well both inside and out with cold water, rub with salt and rinse. Remove membranes and excess fat. Soak in cold, salted water several hours.

2 Turn stomach inside out for stuffing. Cover heart and liver with water in a pot. Bring to a boil, reduce heat, cover and simmer 30 minutes. Chop heart and coarsely grind liver. In a skillet, toast oatmeal, stirring frequently, until golden. Combine remaining ingredients (except Neeps and Tatties) and mix well. Loosely pack mixture into stomach, about one-half to two-thirds full. Press air out of stomach and tie both ends securely with cotton twine. Place into a large pot and completely cover with boiling water. Simmer, uncovered, 3 hours, adding more boiling water if needed to keep haggis covered.

3 Prick stomach several times with a sharp needle when it begins to swell. Place haggis on a platter and remove strings.

4 To serve, cut haggis open with a knife and serve with a spoon with Neeps and Tatties on the side.

SERVES 8 TO 12

Australian Kidney Meat Pie

INGREDIENTS

SHORTCRUST PASTRY:

¾ cup all-purpose flour plus more for dusting

¾ cup self-rising flour

Pinch salt

3½ ounces cold butter

3 tablespoons cold water

1 teaspoon lemon juice

VENISON KIDNEY PIE:

1 ounce venison kidney

3 cups water, divided

Juice of ½ lemon

3 thin slices bacon, chopped

2 onions, sliced

3½ pounds boneless venison steak, cubed small

½ teaspoon dried thyme

1 stick celery, minced

1 teaspoon salt

½ teaspoon pepper

3 tablespoons all-purpose flour

½ cup cold water

1 egg, lightly beaten

3 tablespoons milk

SERVES 6

1 Place flours and salt in mixing bowl and cut in butter with fingertips.

2 Mix in water and lemon juice. Turn out onto lightly floured surface; knead. Let rest 20 minutes in a covered bowl.

VENISON KIDNEY PIE:

3 Cut kidneys open, remove connective tissues and chop fine. Soak 30 minutes in 1 cup water with lemon juice.

4 Fry bacon in a large saucepan. When it begins to sizzle, add onions and sauté over low heat until onions are clear.

5 Add steak, kidney, thyme, celery, salt, pepper, and 2 cups water. Cover and simmer 1½ hours.

6 Preheat oven to 450°. Whisk flour into ½ cup cold water and slowly stir into meat. Continue to stir until thick. Pour into large pie pan. Roll out pastry to ⅛-inch thick and cut off a few strips.

7 Whisk egg into milk and brush edge of pan. Place pastry strips around edge and remaining pastry on top of pie. Trim edges and seal by pressing down with a fork. Make a few steam holes in center and brush with egg mixture.

8 Bake 10 minutes, lower heat to 350° and bake until crust is browned.

Simmered Venison Tongue
with Vegetables

INGREDIENTS

1 onion

4 whole cloves

4 to 5 pounds venison tongue, cleaned

8 leeks, sliced, divided

2 garlic cloves, sliced

7 carrots, in 1-inch pieces, divided

1 rib celery, in ½-inch pieces

1 bay leaf

1 teaspoon thyme

1½ tablespoons salt

1½ teaspoons pepper

6 medium onions, quartered

6 turnips, peeled and quartered

Seasonal vegetables, cooked

Grated fresh horseradish

French-style mustard

Baked potatoes, halved

1 Stick onion with cloves. Place venison tongue, onion, 2 leeks, garlic, 1 carrot, celery, bay leaf and thyme in a large kettle. Fill with water to reach about 2 inches above tongue. Bring to a boil and boil 5 minutes.

2 Remove any foam that rises to the top. Cover and simmer 3½ hours. One hour before it is ready, add salt, pepper and onions. After 20 minutes, add turnips and remaining leeks and carrots.

3 When tongue is tender, transfer to a platter. Carefully remove skin by loosening it at the ends and pulling it off. Trim base of tongue. Return tongue to broth and reheat.

4 Serve on a platter surrounded with seasonal vegetables. Serve with grated fresh horseradish, mustard and potatoes in their skins.

SERVES 4

MARINADES

"Should I or should I not marinate my venison?" The answer is, "Maybe yes or maybe no—it all depends on the type of venison that you have on hand or what you are trying to accomplish." Do you wish to add flavor, tenderize a tough cut of meat, hide a gamey smell—or all three?

I am a meat hunter. I have harvested my share of large-rack deer in my life, but for the last twenty years, I hunt for the table. I choose not to marinate most of my venison, because most are harvested specifically for the table.

1. I try to selectively harvest young-mature deer,

2. I try to harvest my young-mature male deer in the early season before they develop their high level of seasonal hormones, and

3. I try to harvest young-mature female deer in early and late season.

This does not mean that I do not keep a watchful eye out for that once-in-a-lifetime trophy. Also, for the record, I have never found a marinade that will completely mask the wild taste of bucks taken during the rut or deer that have been taken after they have been driven.

For these older male deer, I used to marinate the meat or use a large portion to make highly seasoned sausage. My harvesting and marinating decisions are just personal and they should not influence how you hunt or how you enjoy your outdoor experience.

Even with younger deer that are naturally tender, there are times I wish to depart subtle flavor. On these occasions, I choose a marinade that contains the type of flavors that I wish to infuse into the meat.

Apple Wine Marinade

INGREDIENTS

1 (25-ounce) bottle apple wine

1 large onion, thinly sliced

12 black peppercorns

12 whole cloves

¼ teaspoon ground nutmeg

6 whole allspice

1 bay leaf

¼ teaspoon salt

1. Mix together all ingredients in a 1-gallon zip-close plastic bag.

2. Add a 5- to 6-pound venison roast and refrigerate 8 to 12 hours. Remove venison from marinade.

Lemon Juice and Peanut Oil Marinade

INGREDIENTS

½ cup red wine vinegar

¾ cup teriyaki sauce

¼ cup Worcestershire sauce

½ cup peanut or canola oil

⅓ cup lemon juice

5 garlic cloves, minced

2 tablespoons dry mustard

1. Mix all ingredients and place in a 1-gallon zip-close plastic bag.

2. Place venison in bag, mix well and refrigerate 8 to 12 hours.

Spiced Venison Marinade and Tenderizer

INGREDIENTS

1 quart apple cider vinegar

½ teaspoon chopped onion

2 bay leaves, halved

½ teaspoon ground pepper

1 teaspoon whole cloves

¼ teaspoon ground allspice

1 teaspoon salt

1 Mix all ingredients together.

2 Place venison and marinade in a 1-gallon zip-close plastic bag and refrigerate 3 days.

3 Remove venison from marinade, drain and wipe dry. Discard marinade.

Green Onion and Red Wine Marinade

INGREDIENTS

10 ounces inexpensive red wine

10 ounces red wine vinegar

2 green onions, chopped

1 white onion, chopped

2 (6-inch more or less) cinnamon sticks, halved

6 whole cloves

1 Mix all ingredients and boil 15 minutes. Cool.

2 Place venison and marinade in a 1-gallon zip-close plastic bag and refrigerate overnight.

Ketchup and Mustard Marinade

INGREDIENTS

¼ cup vegetable oil

¼ cup apple cider vinegar

1 tablespoon Worcestershire sauce

¼ cup ketchup

2 cloves garlic, minced

½ teaspoon dry mustard

½ teaspoon salt

⅛ teaspoon black pepper

1 Mix all marinade ingredients.

2 Place marinade and venison in a 1-gallon zip-close plastic bag and refrigerate 6 hours, turning every 2 hours.

3 Remove venison and allow to drain.

4 Makes enough marinade for 4 pounds of venison.

Spiced Grapette Marinade

INGREDIENTS

4 (12-ounce) Grapettes (grape-flavored soft drink)

2 green onions, chopped

2 garlic cloves, chopped fine

¼ teaspoon ground nutmeg

⅛ teaspoon ground ginger

1 Mix all ingredients.

2 Place marinade and venison in 1-gallon zip-close plastic bag and marinate in refrigerator 4 to 6 hours.

3 Remove venison, strain marinade and reserve. Reduce marinade by about one third to one half and serve as a sauce.

"Tough Old Buck" Marinade

Normally, the only reason to marinate quality venison is to depart a particular flavor into the meat. However, this marinade not only has an outstanding flavor, but if you have one of those "Tough Old Buck" roasts that has a strong, wild smell, this marinade recipe "may" help disguise some of the seasonal smell.

INGREDIENTS

- ¾ cup Burgundy or other dry red wine
- ¼ cup balsamic or other vinegar
- 3 tablespoons sorghum molasses or other dark syrup
- 3 tablespoons olive oil
- 3 garlic cloves, minced
- 3 tablespoons orange zest
- 3 tablespoons lemon zest
- 2 tablespoons chopped fresh thyme
- 2 tablespoons chopped fresh rosemary
- 1 tablespoon crushed juniper berries
- 8 whole cloves
- 8 whole peppercorns
- 2 bay leaves, halved
- ¾ teaspoon salt

1 Combine and mix all ingredients.

2 Inject some of the marinade liquid deep into venison roast.

3 Place marinade and venison in either a 1-gallon zip-close plastic bag or a non-reactive container, cover and refrigerate overnight.

This is a fine trophy. But, this older deer will probably be tough and may benefit from "Tough Old Buck" Marinade.

SAUCES

You might ask, "Why would one consider making sauces at deer camp?" The reason is simple. Wild game and, in particular, venison are enhanced by fruits, fruit-flavored sauces, and the earth flavors of mushrooms, cinnamon, nutmeg, cloves, sage, and rosemary.

Take, for instance, the simple little juniper berry. It has been used to flavor wild fowl and game in Old World Europe for hundreds, if not thousands of years. Other fruits that enhance venison are citrus fruits and our native fruits such as blueberries, blackberries, American persimmons, raspberries, cranberries, wild plum, pawpaw, currants, muscadines and their respective jellies, and nuts such as pecan, hickory, walnut, and hazelnut.

I am of the opinion that the reason you see so many wild game marinades that call for rum, bourbon, sherry, port, wine, and fruit liqueurs is because all of these spirits are made from fruits or grains that have relatively high sugar contents. This may also be why wild game responds favorably to sugar, especially unprocessed brown sugar and molasses, and especially sorghum molasses.

You may have never considered making sauces, gravies or salad dressings at deer camp and may have even been reluctant to try your hand at making them at home. The sauces I have worked up for this section are easy to make. Except for a few of the common flour-based gravies that home cooks are familiar with, the sauce recipes in this section are straight forward and within easy reach. Just mix the ingredients together, add a little heat, and you are ready to enjoy your venison dinner in a way you may have never enjoyed it before.

Native Persimmon Sauce

Unripe native American persimmons are very astringent while still on the tree. Gather ripe persimmons from the ground in the early fall.

1 cup native persimmon pulp

1 cup water, more if needed

1 tablespoon lemon juice

2 tablespoons orange-flavored liqueur

¼ teaspoon ground cinnamon

1 Mix ingredients in a saucepan and add more water if needed to thin.

2 Reduce over medium heat to sauce consistency.

Rum and Cinnamon Sauce

The alcohol in the small amount of rum evaporates during heating and leaves a distinctive sugarcane flavor.

INGREDIENTS

½ cup sugar

½ teaspoon ground cinnamon

½ teaspoon cornstarch

2 tablespoons, more or less, inexpensive dark rum

1 Place sugar, cinnamon and 1 cup water in a small saucepan and bring to a boil.

2 Mix cornstarch in 1 teaspoon water and add to pan. Stir until sauce is clear.

3 Remove from heat and stir in rum.

4 Makes about 1 cup.

Blackberry Sauce

This recipe calls for a sieve or hand-turned food mill and few deer camps have these items in the pot drawer. However, these items are very inexpensive and can be purchased at any chain discount store. I would recommend a food mill over a sieve. A hand-turned food mill is much faster.

INGREDIENTS

½ cup blackberries or raspberries, fresh or frozen

¼ cup rice wine vinegar or other mild flavored vinegar

2 tablespoons dark brown sugar

¼ teaspoon ground cinnamon

⅛ teaspoon ground nutmeg

⅛ teaspoon ground cloves

⅛ teaspoon cayenne pepper

¼ teaspoon salt

1 Rub blackberries through a fine sieve or hand-turned food mill.

2 In a small saucepan, combine blackberry juice and remaining ingredients and heat until slightly thickened.

Cream Sauce

INGREDIENTS

3 tablespoons all-purpose flour

1½ cups canned beef broth

6 tablespoons cream

Salt and pepper to taste

1 Whisk flour into beef broth. Pour into a saucepan and cook, stirring, 1 minute or until sauce has thickened. Scrape browned bits from bottom of pan.

2 Add cream and salt and pepper to taste.

Orange Whiskey Sauce

The alcohol in the rum evaporates and leaves a distinctive sugarcane flavor.

INGREDIENTS

1 tablespoon butter, softened

¼ cup finely chopped green onions

10 cranberries, fresh or frozen, crushed

¼ cup rum

¾ cup orange juice

2 tablespoons lemon juice

2 tablespoons red currant jelly

1 teaspoon French-style mustard

2 teaspoons cornstarch

2 tablespoons water

1   Combine butter, green onions and cranberries in a saucepan. Cook over medium heat until onions soften.

2   Add rum and heat until just boiling.

3   Stir in orange and lemon juices, currant jelly and mustard. Heat until boiling.

4   Whisk cornstarch into the water. Slowly stir cornstarch mixture into sauce and cook until thickened. Serve as soon as possible.

Brown Sugar and Spice Sauce

An old sauce recipe from the Ardennes forest area of Belgium.

INGREDIENTS

4 tablespoons all-purpose flour

1 cup packed light brown sugar

1 small onion, chopped fine

¼ teaspoon ground cloves

½ teaspoon ground ginger

½ teaspoon salt

⅛ teaspoon black pepper

1   Mix flour with just enough cold water to make a paste and place in a skillet. Add 1 cup cold water and remaining ingredients; cook over medium heat, stirring constantly, until a smooth sauce is formed.

2   Pour sauce over venison and serve at once.

Sauce Haroldo

An outstanding sauce for any wild red meat and also for wild fowl.

INGREDIENTS

- ¼ cup salt-cured ham, sliced thin and shredded
- 1 cup inexpensive dry white wine
- 1 cup inexpensive dry red wine
- ¾ cup red wine vinegar
- ½ lemon, peeled, sliced and seeded
- 4 cloves garlic, halved
- 6 dried whole juniper berries
- 2 fresh sprigs rosemary
- 2 fresh sprigs parsley
- 2 fresh whole sage leaves
- 4 anchovy fillets, chopped fine
- 2 chicken livers, chopped fine
- Salt and pepper to taste

1 In a large stainless steel or glass cooking pot, mix together ham, wines, vinegar, lemon, garlic, juniper berries, rosemary, parsley and sage. Bring to a boil and boil 5 minutes.

2 Remove garlic, juniper berries, rosemary, parsley and sage.

3 Add anchovies and chicken livers. Simmer over very low heat until sauce is reduced by half. Salt and pepper to taste.

Lemon-Flavored White Sauce

INGREDIENTS

2 tablespoons butter, softened

1½ to 2 tablespoons all-purpose flour

1 cup half-and-half or milk

1 teaspoon lemon juice

1 to 2 teaspoons sherry to taste

1 Melt butter over low heat. Whisk flour into half-and-half and add to butter. Stir slowly and constantly until sauce begins to thicken.

2 Stir in lemon juice and sherry and serve.

Bar-B-Q Sauce

INGREDIENTS

½ cup ketchup

½ cup water

¼ cup apple cider vinegar

¼ cup finely chopped white onion

3 tablespoons packed brown sugar

2 tablespoons Worcestershire sauce

1 tablespoon lime juice

1 tablespoon paprika

1 teaspoon mustard powder

1 teaspoon liquid smoke

¼ teaspoon chili powder

Salt and pepper to taste

1 Mix together all ingredients, bring to a low boil and remove from stove.

2 Allow to set 30 minutes for flavors to blend.

Mustard and Ketchup Sauce

Serve with broiled venison steaks.

INGREDIENTS

¼ cup vegetable oil

¼ cup apple cider vinegar

¼ cup ketchup

1 tablespoon Worcestershire sauce

2 cloves garlic, minced

½ teaspoon dry mustard

½ teaspoon salt

⅛ teaspoon black pepper

1 Mix all ingredients, bring to a boil and boil 10 minutes.

2 Strain and serve on broiled venison steaks.

Hot Mustard Sauce

INGREDIENTS

¼ cup dry mustard

3½ tablespoons cold water

1 Stir together mustard and water until smooth and let stand 5 minutes before serving.

Mushroom and Onion Skillet Gravy

¼ cup finely chopped onion

¼ cup chopped mushrooms

4 tablespoons skillet drippings or melted fat or shortening

1 cup or more cold or room temperature milk

2 tablespoons all-purpose flour

Pinch each salt and pepper

1 teaspoon minced fresh parsley, optional

1 Sauté onion and mushrooms in skillet drippings until onion is just clear.

2 Pour milk into a wide-mouth drinking glass.

3 Mix flour, salt and pepper and pour into milk and briskly whisk to dissolve flour. The flour dissolves, but it will have a tendency to quickly settle to bottom of the glass.

4 Just before pouring milk mixture into skillet, whisk again. Stop pouring when you have about an inch of milk remaining. Shake the glass to dissolve remaining flour and pour into skillet.

5 With spatula, continually keep flour agitated and to prevent it from burning. If gravy thickens more than you wish, quickly stir in more milk.

6 A minute before removing from stove, stir in parsley.

7 If you wish to make this gravy ahead of time, remove skillet from stove and lay a piece of plastic wrap onto surface of gravy. The plastic wrap will prevent air from coming in contact with surface and prevent surface from skimming over.

SERVES 4

The Mississippi Sportsman

FORMERLY THE RESERVOIR NEWS & VIEWS

50¢

BOATING HUNTING CAMPING ENTERTAINMENT FISHING RACING

APPETIZERS

There always seems to be one or two times each year when appetizers are required, appropriate and worth the effort. These times usually are:

- First day of gun season.
- A special celebration.
- Some "high placed" visitor or dignitary.
- Off-season events for the whole family.

I remember the day when our first Bubbaleen camp member harvested, hauled, skinned and butchered her first big buck—all by herself. Now that was an occasion for one fine celebration. We Bubbas had never had any rule against having a Bubbaleen member and had really not given it much thought. Over the years, we have had many daughters, nieces, wives, and girlfriends hunt with us. But, this was the first time that someone had sought us out and specifically asked to become a full member in her own right. There were many things that she did not know, many things that she wanted to know, and she was not shy in asking.

One question that she asked was, "How do you easily lift a big deer onto an ATV all by yourself?" Other than saying, "Come back to camp and get some help," no one had a good answer. At the dinner table later in the year, she asked, "Do you guys want me to teach you how to get a big deer onto an ATV—all by yourself?" It seems that she had been studying the problem and had devised an ingenious method for her to load a deer—all by herself. I suspect all of us had been pondering this same problem for years and, other than asking for help or dragging the deer all the way back to camp

behind a Jeep or ATV, no one had ever come up with a viable solution.

Her solution to the problem was so simple and straightforward that it bordered on the sublime. She backed her ATV up to a tree, stood on the back, reached up as high as she could, and tied a piece of ¼-inch rope around the tree. Then she tied on a small rope hoist. Since we did not have a fresh deer for her to demonstrate with, she used her ATV to pull a bale of hay from the horse barn to the tree. She said, "If this bale of hay was a deer, I would tie the feet together with the other end of the rope and hook the hoist on the tied feet." So instead, she tied the other end of the rope around the bale of hay and used the hoist to pull the bale head-high and tied the hoist rope to the tree. She then backed her ATV under the bale, lowered it onto the rear rack, reached up and untied the hoist from the tree and she was done. And, she did it in ten minutes and without even breaking a sweat. It was as simple as that. Now if that piece of hunting genius did not call for a proper celebration, nothing ever would. Within a week, every one of us Bubbas had a rig similar to hers tucked away in our ATVs or Korean War–era vintage Jeeps.

Bubbaleen's Ingenious Single-Handed Tree Hoist—Mine is Still in Use Twenty Years Later

Over the years, I must have assembled and given away at least twenty or thirty of these tree hoists. There was a day when I could load a small deer on the back of a pickup truck all by myself. I now find it is becoming increasingly more difficult to lift heavy objects, so I rely on what that young Bubbaleen taught me that day more than twenty years ago.

Miss Anne's Black-Eyed Pea New Year's Dip

1 (14-ounce) can black-eyed peas, drained and rinsed

1 cup mayonnaise

1 cup sour cream

2 (.4-ounce) packages dry buttermilk ranch dressing mix

1 (14-ounce) can artichoke hearts, drained and chopped

2 medium onions, chopped fine

4 tablespoons grated Parmesan cheese

2 cups grated mozzarella cheese, divided

1 Preheat oven to 350°. Mix together first 7 ingredients with 1 cup mozzarella. Pour into an ovenproof baking dish or pie plate.

2 Top with remaining 1 cup mozzarella. Bake until heated.

3 Serve with chips or on toasted bread.

SERVES 15 TO 25

Rolled Venison Appetizers

2 pounds venison loin, sliced less than ½-inch thick

Salt and pepper to taste

½ pound spicy venison or bulk pork sausage

4 medium carrots, julienned

Natural wood toothpicks

All-purpose flour

1 Pound loin thin and cut into 3- to 4-inch squares. Sprinkle with salt and pepper and spread with sausage. Place several pieces of carrot on each. Roll and secure with a toothpick. Dust with flour.

2 Heat a little shortening in an ovenproof pan and brown the rolls. Partly cover with water, cover and bake at 350° for 1½ to 2 hours or until tender.

SERVES 6

Thin-Sliced Loin Appetizer
with Sour Cream Onion Dip

INGREDIENTS

Venison loin

Cotton twine

Vegetable oil

4 green onions

1 (16-ounce) container sour
  cream

Salt

White or black pepper

Prepared honey mustard

Natural wooden toothpicks

1 Preheat oven to 350°. Tie loin every inch with cotton twine and coat with vegetable oil. Place on rack in roasting pan and roast to internal temperature of 138°, about 30 to 45 minutes.

2 While loin is roasting, finely chop white part of green onions and mix into sour cream. Mix in salt and pepper to taste.

3 Slice 1 tablespoon green onion tops and sprinkle on top of sour cream. Refrigerator sour cream mixture until ready to serve.

4 When internal temperature of loin reaches 138°, remove from oven, wrap in foil and allow to rest 15 minutes before slicing thin.

5 Spread a little honey mustard on each slice, roll and secure with a toothpick. Serve with sour cream mixture on the side.

Mexican Venison Crockpot Appetizer

2 pounds Velveeta, cubed

1 (16-ounce) can enchilada sauce

1 (15-ounce) can chili without beans

2 pounds ground venison

1 large yellow onion, chopped

2 tablespoons cooking oil or skillet drippings

1 (6-ounce) jar jalapeño peppers, chopped and drained

Tortilla chips

1 Mix together Velveeta, enchilada sauce and chili. Cook in a crockpot over low heat until cheese melts. Stir often.

2 In a skillet, brown venison and onion in hot oil and add to crockpot. Stir in chopped jalapeños. Cook on low 1 hour.

3 Serve with tortilla chips.

SERVES 4

Simple Venison Roll Hors D'oeuvres

½ (17.3-ounce) box refrigerated Pepperidge Farm puff pastry sheets

All-purpose flour

1 pound bulk venison breakfast sausage

1 egg white

1 Preheat oven to 425°. Remove 1 pastry sheet from refrigerator and let stand until just softened. Pastry must be cold enough to hold together. Roll pastry sheet out on lightly floured surface to about 14x11-inches. If pastry becomes too soft, place it back in refrigerator 10 minutes. Use as little flour as possible because too much will make the pastry taste like flour.

2 Flour your hands and roll venison sausage on a lightly floured surface until it is almost as long as the long side of pastry rectangle.

3 Brush sausage with egg white and lay sausage along long edge of pastry. Roll up in the pastry and brush with egg white to seal.

4 Slice roll every 3 to 4 inches to make little individual sausage roundels. Place roundels on foil-covered cookie sheet and bake 10 to 20 minutes or until brown on top.

SERVES 4

Teriyaki Fondue

INGREDIENTS

1 tablespoon teriyaki sauce

1 tablespoon water

2 tablespoons sugar

¼ teaspoon instant minced onion

⅛ teaspoon garlic salt

⅛ teaspoon MSG, optional

⅛ teaspoon ground ginger

½ pound ground venison or venison burger

½ cup fine soft breadcrumbs, unseasoned

Bamboo skewers

Cooking oil

Ketchup

Dijon mustard

1 Combine first 7 ingredients; let stand 10 minutes.

2 Mix venison and breadcrumbs; stir in teriyaki mixture. Shape into ¾-inch meat balls. Refrigerate until serving time.

3 Spear meat balls onto bamboo skewers. Heat oil in a fondue pot and cook meat balls until well browned.

4 Serve with heated ketchup and mustard.

MAKES ABOUT 30

Marinated Venison Strips

1 pound venison roast, cooked rare

1 small onion, sliced into thin rings

¾ teaspoon salt

Dash pepper

1½ tablespoons fresh lemon juice

1 cup sour cream

Lettuce

1 Cut venison into thin strips. Separate onion into rings.

2 Combine venison, onion, salt and pepper. Sprinkle with lemon juice, stir in sour cream and chill.

3 Serve in lettuce-lined dishes.

SERVES 6

Link Sausage Appetizers
in Red Wine Sauce

2 pounds link venison sausage

3 tablespoons butter, softened

1 bunch green onions, white and green parts chopped

1½ cups inexpensive red wine

Salt and pepper to taste

½ cup chopped parsley

1 Cut sausage links into 2-inch lengths. Heat a skillet and melt butter. Brown sausage on all sides. Halfway through cooking add green onions.

2 Add red wine, cover and bring to a boil. Reduce heat and simmer 45 minutes to 1 hour. Salt and pepper to taste.

3 Place in a chaffing dish, sprinkle with parsley and serve hot.

SERVES 4 TO 6

BREAD

I like bread and I especially like bread with my venison. But, I also like to sit around the fire in my shorts, in my ragged over-stuffed lounge chair, and prop my feet up on my deer-hide-covered stool. To me, cooking at deer camp should not be a chore and making traditional white loaf bread is a chore. When I am supposed to be having fun, baking traditional loaf white bread is more work than I am willing to do.

Some years ago, when I stumbled onto a recipe for Sally Lunn Hot Bread (page 163), I immediately realized that I had found the perfect white bread recipe for deer camp. There is nothing fancy about Sally Lunn Hot Bread—except that it is easy to make and tastes downright good. I am normally a very sharing person, but when I am served this bread, hot out of the oven and slathered with real homemade butter, I could eat the whole loaf.

I grew up eating my grandmother's handmade biscuits for breakfast every morning. The only time I can get handmade biscuits these days is at deer camp. Those plastic bags of frozen, premade, "old-fashioned" biscuits you purchase at the grocery store are just okay, but they are not the same as real biscuits. In keeping with the concept of the "cooking creatively at deer camp" theme of this book, I modified an old family biscuit recipe that serves as an all-in-one breakfast. With the Bacon, Cheese and Green Onion Biscuits recipe (page 168), the only other things you need to get you off and going on a brisk morning in the woods are dry socks, warm boots, and a hot cup of coffee.

Bacon, Cheese and Green Onion Biscuits

On occasion, I have been known to poke my finger into the side of several of these biscuits, pour in some syrup and melted butter, wrap them in aluminum foil, and carry them along with me. For a proper gourmet brunch in my tree stand, the only other thing that I need is a thermos full of hot chocolate and I am good until dinner. Another bread that I like to wrap in aluminum foil and carry along with me to my tree stand is Applesauce and Sorghum Molasses Bread (page 166). In ¾-inch-thick slices, it holds together fine. Since this is a sweet bread, rather than my normal hot chocolate I fill my thermos with black coffee.

If I say nothing else that might encourage you to bake some bread at deer camp, I encourage you to try your hand at some of these recipes. They are all well worth the effort and at the meat-dividing-up-time, your efforts may even get you an extra backstrap (loin) from your friends. Or maybe not if I am around.

Sally Lunn Hot Bread

A slightly sweet, light bread commonly used by early settlers in the American West.

1 (.25-ounce) package dry yeast

1 cup lukewarm water

⅓ cup whole milk

1 cup butter, melted

4 eggs, well beaten

3 tablespoons sugar

1 tablespoon salt

4 cups sifted all-purpose flour

1 Soften yeast in lukewarm water. Heat milk to lukewarm and add it and melted butter to eggs.

2 Add sugar, salt, yeast mixture and flour. Mix well. Pour in a bowl, cover and let double in size.

3 When risen, beat batter well and pour into an oiled angel food cake pan. Allow to rise 1½ hours.

4 Preheat oven to 350°. Bake 25 minutes. Serve hot.

SERVES 4 TO 6

Farmhouse Bread

Simple to make and tastes even better.

1 (.25-ounce) package dry yeast

2 cups lukewarm water

3¾ cups all-purpose flour, divided

1 cup whole-wheat flour

1 teaspoon sugar

½ teaspoon salt

4 tablespoons butter, melted

1 In a small bowl, sprinkle yeast over lukewarm water and stir to dissolve.

2 Mix 3½ cups flour, whole-wheat flour, sugar and salt in a large bowl. Stir in yeast mixture.

3 Turn dough out onto a lightly floured surface. Knead 10 minutes until smooth and springy, adding only enough of remaining flour to keep dough from sticking. Shape into a round loaf.

4 Set loaf on lightly floured baking sheet. Cover with a cloth and let rise in a warm place 1 hour.

5 Preheat oven to 425°. Gently brush risen dough with melted butter. Wait a minute or 2 and sprinkle lightly with flour. Bake 10 minutes.

6 Lower heat to 400° and bake 20 minutes, or until bread is lightly browned and sounds hollow when bottom or sides are tapped.

SERVES 4 TO 6

Applesauce and Sorghum Molasses Bread

½ cup butter, softened

1 cup sugar

3 eggs

2 cups all-purpose flour

1 teaspoon baking powder

½ teaspoon salt

½ teaspoon ground cinnamon

¼ teaspoon ground nutmeg

1 cup applesauce

¼ cup sorghum molasses or other dark syrup

1 cup raisins

½ cup chopped walnuts, hickory nuts or pecans

1 Preheat oven to 350°. With an electric mixer, cream butter and sugar until light and fluffy.

2 Add eggs, 1 at a time, and beat after each addition.

3 Sift together flour, baking powder, salt, cinnamon and nutmeg and set aside.

4 Mix together applesauce and molasses. Alternating dry and wet, add flour and applesauce mixtures to egg mixture and mix well after each addition.

5 Fold in raisins and nuts. Pour into a greased 9¼x5½x2¾-inch loaf pan.

6 Place pan on middle rack of oven and bake 1 hour. Test with a toothpick until it comes out clean. Remove pan from oven and allow to cool 10 minutes. Remove bread from pan and cool on wire rack.

SERVES 4

Country Yeast Biscuits

2 (.25-ounce) packages dry yeast

¼ cup warm water

2 cups buttermilk, room temperature

5 cups all-purpose flour plus more for dusting

¼ cup sugar

1 tablespoon baking powder

1 tablespoon baking soda

1 teaspoon salt

1 cup lard or vegetable shortening

1 Preheat oven to 450°. Combine yeast and warm water and let stand 10 minutes.

2 Combine yeast mixture with buttermilk and set aside.

3 Sift together flour, sugar, baking powder, baking soda and salt. Cut lard into dry mixture until it resembles coarse meal.

4 Add buttermilk mixture to dry ingredients and gently stir with a fork until dry ingredients are moistened.

5 Turn biscuit dough out onto a lightly floured surface and gently knead only 3 or 4 times.

6 Roll dough ¾-inch thick and cut straight down (do not twist) with a 2½- to 3-inch biscuit cutter. Place biscuits on lightly greased baking sheet. Cover and let rise in a warm place 1 hour.

7 Bake 10 to 12 minutes or until golden brown.

SERVES 8

Bacon, Cheese and Green Onion Biscuits

4 slices smoked bacon

½ cup vegetable shortening

2 cups self-rising flour plus more for dusting

½ cup (2-ounces) shredded sharp Cheddar cheese

¾ cup plus 2 tablespoons whole milk

¼ cup chopped green onions

1 Preheat oven to 450°. Cook, drain and crumble bacon and set aside.

2 Cut vegetable shortening into flour until mixture resembles coarse meal.

3 Add cheese, milk, onions and cooked bacon. Stir until dry ingredients are moistened.

4 Turn dough out onto lightly floured surface and knead only 3 or 4 times.

5 Roll out dough ¾-inch thick. Cut straight down with a biscuit cutter (do not twist) and place biscuits, with edges touching, on ungreased baking sheet. Bake 10 to 12 minutes.

SERVES 4 TO 6

Pappy's Hushpuppies for 30 to 40

Adapted from a recipe by Mr. Carlton Allen. This recipe can be halved to make hush-puppies for 15 to 20.

INGREDIENTS

5 pounds white onions, chopped

6 green bell peppers, chopped

1½ cups sugar

2 teaspoons cayenne pepper

2 cups self-rising flour

10 cups self-rising cornmeal

½ cup white vinegar

4 eggs, beaten

Peanut oil

TO MAKE BATTER:

1 Mix onions and bell peppers together. In batches, purée in a food processor until liquefied and set aside.

2 Sift together sugar, pepper, flour and cornmeal.

3 Mix together all ingredients except peanut oil, cover and refrigerate overnight.

TO COOK:

4 Heat peanut oil in a deep-fat fryer or a large cast-iron cooking pot until oil reaches 375°. Drop 1 heaping tablespoon dough into hot oil and cook until golden brown.

5 Do not crowd hushpuppies as they will swell while cooking. Fry in small batches and allow to drain between layers of paper towels.

SERVES 30 TO 40

Tex-Mex Buttermilk Cornbread

¼ cup chopped onion

1 tablespoon butter

2 jalapeños, seeded and diced

½ cup fresh or canned corn kernels

¼ cup chopped pimento

1 cup all-purpose flour

½ teaspoon baking soda

1½ teaspoons baking powder

1½ tablespoons sugar

1 teaspoon salt

2 cups cornmeal

1½ cups buttermilk

2 eggs, lightly beaten

3 tablespoons butter, melted

1 Preheat oven to 425°. Sauté onion in butter until just clear. Remove from heat and add jalapeños, corn and pimento.

2 In a bowl, sift together flour, baking soda, baking powder, sugar and salt. Stir in cornmeal.

3 In another bowl, combine buttermilk, eggs and melted butter.

4 Combine corn mixture with buttermilk mixture. Mix with dry ingredients.

5 Pour into a greased 9x9-inch pan and bake 25 to 30 minutes.

SERVES 4 TO 6

Brown Sugar Cornbread

Some say that lard in our food is not good for us. Some others would argue that until the 1940's everybody cooked with lard and it was not considered unhealthy. If you have never eaten cornbread that is made with lard, the difference in taste will surprise you. However, if you are concerned, you can substitute vegetable shortening in this recipe for the lard.

INGREDIENTS

¾ cup all-purpose flour, sifted

3½ teaspoons double-acting baking powder

4 tablespoons packed dark brown or raw sugar

¾ teaspoon salt

1¼ cups yellow cornmeal

1 egg, lightly beaten

¼ cup lard or vegetable shortening, melted

1 cup whole milk

Real butter, softened

1 Preheat oven to 425°. Grease an 8x8-inch heavy pan or cast-iron skillet. Place pan in oven until sizzling hot.

2 Sift together flour, baking powder, sugar, salt and cornmeal.

3 Combine egg, melted lard and milk and pour into flour mixture. Stir just enough to moisten dry ingredients. Do not beat.

4 Carefully pour batter into hot pan and bake about 30 minutes, or until golden.

5 Remove cornbread from pan, cut into squares, place a large pat of butter between squares and serve immediately.

6 Note: A proper cornbread should be 1½-inches thick. To make thicker cornbread, use a smaller pan.

SERVES 4 TO 6

Irish Whiskey-Flavored Breakfast Muffins

INGREDIENTS

DRY INGREDIENTS:

2 cups all-purpose flour

½ cup sugar

1 tablespoon baking powder

½ teaspoon salt

WET INGREDIENTS:

1 egg, beaten

½ cup butter, melted

½ cup cream

¼ cup coffee liqueur

¼ cup Irish whiskey

1 Preheat oven to 400°. Sift together dry ingredients.

2 Mix wet ingredients together and slowly stir into dry ingredients.

3 Line a muffin pan with paper liners and pour in batter two-thirds full. Bake 20 minutes.

MAKES 12

Apricot-Pecan Deer Camp Muffins

INGREDIENTS

- 10 paper muffin cup liners
- 1 cup buttermilk
- 1 cup bran
- 1½ cups unsifted all-purpose flour
- 1 teaspoon baking soda
- ½ teaspoon ground cinnamon
- ¼ teaspoon salt
- ⅓ cup butter, softened
- ½ cup sugar
- 1 large egg
- 1 teaspoon vanilla extract
- ¾ cup chopped dried apricots
- ½ cup chopped pecans, walnuts, hickory nuts, hazelnuts, almonds or a combination

1 Preheat oven to 400°. Spray insides of paper liners with nonstick spray and place in a muffin pan.

2 In small bowl, combine buttermilk and bran and set aside.

3 Combine flour, baking soda, cinnamon and salt and set aside.

4 In large bowl, by hand or with an electric mixer, beat butter and sugar until light and fluffy. Add egg and vanilla extract; beat until well blended.

5 With mixer speed on low, add flour and buttermilk mixtures to butter mixture. Beat just until batter is blended. Stir in apricots and nuts.

6 Spoon batter into muffin cup liners. Bake 20 to 25 minutes.

7 Remove liners from muffin pan and allow to cool 5 to 10 minutes. Remove muffins from paper liners.

MAKES 10

Cornmeal Buttermilk Pancakes

The very pronounced cornmeal taste may be too intense for some

INGREDIENTS

1 cup yellow cornmeal

2 teaspoons sugar

1 teaspoon salt

2 eggs, well beaten

1⅓ cups buttermilk

Butter

1 Mix cornmeal, sugar and salt. In a separate bowl, mix eggs and buttermilk. Combine mixtures; beat until smooth.

2 Heat and grease a griddle or large, heavy skillet. Pour in 2 to 3 tablespoons batter for each pancake.

3 Cook until brown around the edges and bubbles appear on top. Turn and cook until bottom begins to brown.

4 Place a pat of butter on each pancake.

MAKES ABOUT 24

Lemon-Blueberry Pancakes

INGREDIENTS

1 egg, well beaten

¾ cup milk

2 tablespoons vegetable oil

1 teaspoon lemon juice

2 teaspoons grated lemon peel

1 cup all-purpose flour

1 tablespoon sugar

1 tablespoon baking powder

½ teaspoon salt

½ cup blueberries

Butter

1 Into beaten egg, beat remaining ingredients except blueberries.

2 Gently stir in blueberries. Heat and grease a griddle or large, heavy skillet. Pour in 3 to 4 tablespoons batter for each pancake.

3 Cook until brown around the edges and bubbles appear on top. Turn and cook until bottom begins to brown.

4 Place a pat of butter on each pancake.

SERVES 4

Applesauce Pancakes
with Apple Cider Syrup

INGREDIENTS

APPLE CIDER SYRUP:

1 tablespoon butter

2 cups apple juice or cider

1 cup brown sugar

2 cinnamon sticks

APPLESAUCE PANCAKES:

2 cups all-purpose flour

¼ cup dark brown sugar

2 tablespoons baking powder

1 teaspoon salt

1 cup milk

½ cup applesauce

¼ cup butter, melted

2 eggs, lightly beaten

APPLE CIDER SYRUP:

1 Melt butter in a saucepan. Stir in apple juice, brown sugar and cinnamon sticks. Bring to a gentle boil, stir and reduce mixture to about 1 cup. Syrup will thicken as it cools.

2 Remove cinnamon sticks and set syrup aside.

APPLESAUCE PANCAKES:

3 Sift together flour, sugar, baking powder and salt.

4 Mix together milk, applesauce, butter and eggs. Mix wet ingredients into dry ingredients.

5 Heat and lightly grease a griddle or large, heavy skillet. Pour in 3 to 4 tablespoons batter per pancake. When bubbles appear on top and edges brown, turn pancakes and cook until bottom begins to brown.

6 Stack pancakes and place a pat of butter between each. Serve with Apple Cider Syrup.

SERVES 6

Banana Waffles
with Banana Syrup

BANANA SYRUP:

½ cup maple or other light syrup

1 cup mashed bananas

1 teaspoon banana extract

1 tablespoon lemon juice

BANANA WAFFLES:

2 cups sifted all-purpose flour

3 teaspoons baking powder

1 tablespoon sugar

½ teaspoon salt

3 eggs, separated

1½ cups milk

5 tablespoons vegetable shortening, melted

1 banana, sliced thin and quartered

Butter

BANANA SYRUP:

1 Heat syrup and bananas in small saucepan 3 minutes.

2 Remove from heat and stir in banana extract and lemon juice. Set aside.

BANANA WAFFLES:

3 Mix together and sift flour, baking powder, sugar and salt.

4 Beat egg yolks and stir in milk and shortening. Mix in dry ingredients and beat until smooth. Stir in banana.

5 Stiffly beat egg whites and fold in.

6 Heat and grease a hot waffle iron. Spoon batter onto waffle iron and cook until brown.

7 Place a pat of butter on each hot waffle and serve with Banana Syrup.

SERVES 4 TO 6

Homemade Dog Biscuits

Homemade dog biscuits are a great Christmas present for Bubba or Bubbaleen's favorite ol' deer dog. Although this recipe is written for the dogs, some people find them better tasting than many health food crackers. If you are cooking these for yourself, you may wish to add a little salt and pepper or possibly some brown sugar or molasses. These dog biscuits are bone-hard and, so that you do not break a tooth, you may wish to soak them in coffee.

INGREDIENTS

3½ cups all-purpose flour

2 cups whole-wheat flour

1 cup rye flour

1½ cups cornmeal, divided

2 cups bulgur (or cracked) wheat

½ cup nonfat dry milk powder

4 teaspoons salt

1 (¼-ounce) package active dry yeast

¼ cup lukewarm water

2 cups canned beef or chicken broth

1 egg

1 tablespoon whole milk

1 Preheat oven to 300°. In a large bowl, sift flours, 1 cup cornmeal, bulgur wheat, milk powder and salt.

2 In a separate bowl, dissolve yeast in lukewarm water and let sit 10 minutes.

3 Add broth to yeast mixture and mix well. Add yeast-broth liquid to flour mixture and knead 3 minutes. The dough should be stiff.

4 Flour a board with ½ cup cornmeal and roll out dough ¼ inch thick. Cut out biscuits with a dog-bone-shaped cutter or round cookie cutter or slice into ½x4-inch long strips. Place on ungreased cookie sheets.

5 Whisk together egg and milk and brush tops of biscuits. Bake 45 minutes. Turn off heat and leave biscuits in oven overnight.

6 The next day biscuits will be bone-hard.

MAKES SEVERAL DOZEN BISCUITS

Hounds and Horses

In my youth, there were very few deer in the state where I grew up. My dad was born in 1915 in a dirt-poor part of the state and he never harvested a deer until 1984. This lack of deer was the result of intensive market hunting that was conducted across the eastern and southern part of the country in the latter part of the 19th century and continued into the early part of the 20th century. Market hunting eliminated virtually all of the native deer population. After market hunting was banned around 1918, the only way country folk and subsistence farmers could harvest a deer to feed their families was to hunt together and divide the meat.

Some camps still use the old technique of driving deer on horseback and with dogs.

In some parts of the country, this tradition of loosing a few deer dogs and a few men riding horses through the woods to drive the deer continues today. Although not as popular today, this was the way I learned to hunt

in my youth. Although most of my deer hunting today is done from a tree stand or a ground blind and over a food plot, the sound of a baying hound echoing through the cold morning fog and hearing a distant rider beating a tin plate can still raise the hair on the back of my neck.

SOUPS

We like soups at home and there is no reason that soups cannot be made and enjoyed at deer camp. Soups are easy to make and they are the classic one-pot meal. All you need to make a complete dinner at camp is a large pot, soup and a loaf of bread or box of salted crackers.

Another nice thing about soups at deer camp is they often taste better the next day or after they have been frozen, thawed and reheated. Most soups can be made rather quickly, but one cannot make really good gumbo or chili and be in a rush.

I can make a fine soup in an hour or so, but I have been known to take all afternoon and sometimes into the evening to make a gumbo for the next day. On occasion, I make a large batch of soup not knowing when I will use it or to whom it will be served. Since soups have such a long shelf life in the freezer, I fill half-gallon plastic containers with the soup and place the containers in the freezer. Once frozen, I remove the frozen block of soup from the plastic container, place it in a large zip-close bag or vacuum package it and return it to the freezer. Whenever we have unexpected guests around dinner time or just don't feel like cooking, it is easy to pull out a package of soup, thaw it in a cooking pot full of boiling water and we have an instant dinner for 4 to 6.

Hearty Vegetable, Ground Venison and Sausage Soup

INGREDIENTS

1 pound ground venison

4 cups cold water

1 (14.5-ounce) can Italian-style stewed tomatoes, undrained

4 tablespoon beef bouillon granules

1½ cups frozen mixed vegetables

1 cup uncooked large macaroni

6 ounces smoked venison sausage, sliced ½ inch thick

Salt and pepper to taste

1 Brown ground venison until just pink, remove and set aside.

2 While venison is browning, combine water, tomatoes with liquid, bouillon granules and vegetables in a pot and bring to a boil.

3 Mix in raw macaroni and browned venison; return to a boil. Reduce heat, cover and simmer 10 minutes, stirring frequently.

4 Mix in venison and simmer 5 more minutes. Season to taste with salt and pepper.

SERVES 4

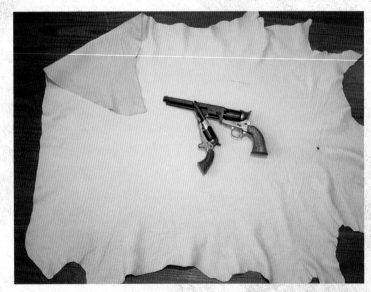

Neck-Shot and Tanned Whitetail Deer Hide

Vegetable and Shank Soup

3 pounds venison shanks with meat (osso buco), cut in 2-inch pieces

1 (16-ounce) can tomato juice

⅓ cup chopped onion

4 teaspoons salt

2 tablespoons Worcestershire sauce

¼ teaspoon chili powder

2 bay leaves

6 cups cold water

1 (16-ounce) can tomatoes

1 cup diced celery

1 (8.75-ounce) can whole-kernel corn

1 cup sliced carrots

1 cup diced potatoes

1 (10-ounce) package frozen lima beans

1 Combine venison, tomato juice, onion, seasonings and water in a soup pot. Cover and simmer 2 hours. Skim foam as needed.

2 Allow to cool and cut meat from bones in large cubes. Strain broth and skim off excess fat.

3 Add meat and vegetables to the pot, cover and simmer 1 hour. Remove bay leaves before serving.

SERVES 8

Ground Venison Vegetable Soup

2 tablespoons vegetable oil

2 pounds ground venison

1 cup diced onion

1 cup cubed potatoes

1 cup sliced carrots

1 cup shredded cabbage

1½ quarts cold water

¼ cup uncooked short-grain rice

4 cups beef concentrate to taste

1 bay leaf

½ teaspoon thyme

2 teaspoons salt

⅛ teaspoon white pepper

1 (28-ounce) can tomatoes, quartered

1 Heat oil in a stockpot or large Dutch oven and brown venison and onion.

2 Add potatoes, carrots, cabbage and water. Bring to a boil.

3 Stir in all remaining ingredients except tomatoes. Cover and simmer over low heat 1 hour. Skim off foam.

4 Add tomatoes and remove bay leaf just prior to serving.

SERVES 8

Chunky Venison Vegetable Soup

2 pounds venison stew meat, cut in ½-inch pieces

2 tablespoons vegetable oil

1 cup chopped onion

6 to 8 ribs celery, sliced in ½-inch pieces

3 cloves garlic, crushed

2 bay leaves

2 teaspoons thyme

1 (14.5-ounce) can diced tomatoes

1 medium carrot, diced

2 medium potatoes, diced

4 cups beef broth

4 cups water

Salt and pepper to taste

3 tablespoons uncooked brown rice

1 Brown venison in oil in skillet. Transfer beef to slow cooker.

2 To skillet, add onion, celery and garlic. Cook, stirring, about 10 minutes or until celery is tender. Transfer cooked vegetables to slow cooker with venison.

3 Add a little water to hot skillet; stir to scrape bottom and remove any browned bits. Add this water to slow cooker.

4 Stir in bay leaves, thyme, tomatoes, carrot, potatoes, broth, 4 cups water and salt and pepper. Cover and cook on low 6 to 8 hours.

5 About 45 minutes before serving, turn slow cooker to high and add rice. Remove bay leaves before serving.

SERVES 4 TO 6

Ground Venison and Black-Eyed Pea Soup

2 tablespoons cooking oil

1 pound ground venison

1 medium onion, chopped

2 garlic cloves, minced

2 medium carrots, diced

2 cups beef broth

2 cups chopped turnip greens
  or cabbage leaves

1 (14.5 ounce) can diced
  tomatoes, undrained

1 (15-ounce) can black-eyed
  peas, drained and rinsed

1 cup canned corn

½ teaspoon salt

¼ teaspoon pepper

Cornbread or corn muffins

1 Heat oil in a small stockpot over medium-low heat. Add venison and onion; sauté, stirring, until venison is just brown.

2 Add garlic and carrots and cook 1 minute longer. Add beef broth and bring to a boil. Simmer 10 minutes.

3 Add the greens, tomatoes, peas, corn and seasonings. Cover and simmer 20 to 25 minutes.

4 Serve with cornbread or corn muffins.

SERVES 4

Chicken and Sausage Gumbo

1 to 1½ pounds venison link sausage, sliced thick

1 cup vegetable oil or lard, divided

1 whole chicken, chopped in 2- to 3-inch pieces with bones

Salt to taste

Cayenne pepper to taste

1 cup all-purpose flour

3 cups chopped onions

2 cups chopped celery

1 cup chopped green bell pepper

1 tablespoon chopped garlic

2 quarts chicken stock or canned chicken broth, warmed

½ cup chopped parsley

1 teaspoon salt

⅛ teaspoon hot sauce, optional

Cooked rice for 6 to 8

Filé powder

Green onions, sliced

1   In a 6- to 8-quart heavy stockpot, sauté sausage in ¼ cup oil. Remove sausage and set aside.

2   Season chicken with salt and cayenne, and brown in the same pot. Set aside.

3   In a large skillet, make a roux by mixing remaining ¾ cup oil and flour. Cook over low heat, stirring constantly to prevent flour from burning. The idea is to very slowly brown the roux until it is a medium brown color. If flour burns, discard it and start over. This may take ½ to 1 hour.

4   When roux is ready, add vegetables. Cook for a minute, stirring, until a glaze forms on vegetables. Place in a large pot along with venison and chicken.

5   Stir in stock, a little at a time. Bring to a gentle boil. Add parsley, 1 teaspoon salt, pinch of cayenne pepper and hot sauce, if using. This should be about half of the required seasoning. Reduce the heat, cover and simmer 2 to 4 hours. Check seasoning and add more salt and pepper to taste.

6   Serve over rice, season with filé powder and top with green onions. The gumbo will be better if it is refrigerated overnight and reheated.

SERVES 6 TO 8

Sausage and Chicken Gumbo over Rice

When I was younger, I wondered what exotic country filé powder came from. Later in life, I learned that "exotic country" was my own backyard. The fresh leaves on a Sassafras tree are hung to dry, then ground into a very fine powder. Some say that filé powder has a subtle and distinct flavor. I am not sure I can say that, but it sure does improve a gumbo or a soup.

INGREDIENTS

HOT CHICKEN BONE STOCK:

Bones from 10 deboned chicken thighs, halved or cracked (save meat for Gumbo, next page)

2½ quarts water

ROUX:

¾ cup canola or other cooking oil, or bacon drippings

1½ cups all-purpose flour, sifted

2 cups coarsely chopped white or yellow onions

½ cup sliced celery, ¼ inch thick

½ cup finely chopped green bell pepper

1 tablespoon garlic, minced fine

1 pound fresh or frozen okra, sliced ½ inch thick

STOCK:

1 Simmer bones in water 1 hour. Skim, strain and discard bones. If needed, add more water to stock to restore the volume to 2½ quarts. Set aside.

ROUX:

2 Add oil to a very large cast-iron skillet and warm over low heat. Slowly stir in flour. Cook over low heat 20 to 30 minutes, stirring and scraping frequently with a flat-ended wooden stirrer until light chocolate brown. Be very careful not to let flour burn. If flour burns, discard it and start over.

3 Remove roux from the heat to stop browning and stir in onions, celery, bell pepper and garlic; stir until vegetables begin to glaze. The roux will darken after vegetables are added.

4 Mix in okra and allow mixture to rest in the skillet 10 minutes.

SOUPS, STEWS & CHILIS

GUMBO:

- 2½ quarts Hot Chicken Bone Stock (previous page) or hot water
- 2 tablespoons finely chopped, gently packed parsley
- 3 bay leaves, halved
- 1¼ teaspoons ground thyme
- 2 tablespoons salt
- 1 teaspoon black pepper
- ⅛ teaspoon cayenne or red pepper or to taste
- 1 teaspoon Tabasco sauce or to taste
- 3 tablespoons Worcestershire sauce
- 4 large tomatoes, skinned and chopped large or canned tomatoes
- 2 pounds medium to hot venison sausage, sliced ½ inch thick
- 10 chicken thighs, skinned, deboned and meat quartered

FOR RICE:

- 3 cups water
- 1 teaspoon salt
- 1½ cups long-grain white rice

TO SERVE:

- ½ cup finely chopped green onions
- Filé powder, ⅛ teaspoon or more per bowl
- Salt and pepper, at table to taste
- Tabasco sauce, at table to taste

GUMBO:

5 Combine roux mixture and broth in a 12-quart stockpot. Add spices; simmer over low heat 30 minutes, stirring occasionally.

6 Add tomatoes, sausage and chicken. Simmer, partially covered, over low heat 1½ to 2 hours until chicken begins to separate, stirring occasionally.

7 Remove from heat and rest 10 to 15 minutes. Soak up any surface grease with paper towels; discard. The gumbo can now be served but will be much better if refrigerated overnight. May also be frozen.

FOR RICE:

8 Bring water to a boil; add rice and salt and stir. Return to a boil, cover, reduce heat to very low, and cook 20 minutes. Do not lift lid while rice is cooking.

TO SERVE:

9 Mound ⅔-cup rice in a large soup bowl. Top with 1 cup gumbo. Sprinkle with chopped onions. Offer filé powder, salt, pepper and Tabasco at the table.

SERVES 10

Corn and Sausage Chowder

1 Polish-style or other venison sausage, cut into thin slices

6 bacon slices, chopped

1 cup chopped onion

¼ cup all-purpose flour

2 cups canned beef or chicken broth

1 cup cold water

4 cups whole-kernel corn

2 cups cubed potatoes

⅛ teaspoon white pepper

Tabasco sauce to taste

2 cups whole milk

4 tablespoons real butter, divided

1 In a soup pot, brown sausage and bacon until bacon is crisp. Remove sausage and bacon; drain on paper towels.

2 Discard all but 2 tablespoons drippings in pan. Sauté onion until just clear.

3 In a stockpot, gradually sift and stir flour into broth and water.

4 Add sausage and bacon, onion, corn, potatoes and white pepper. Add Tabasco to taste. Heat to boiling.

5 Reduce heat, cover and simmer 15 to 20 minutes. Stir occasionally.

6 Add milk and cook until soup is heated and potatoes are tender.

7 Serve in individual bowls topped with a dollop of butter.

SERVES 6 TO 8

STEWS

In thinking about this section, I am reminded of dear ol' Mary Simms. When my parents passed away, I "retired" and moved across country from Las Vegas to my parents' retirement home in Mississippi. It was a bittersweet move. Since I moved away from Mississippi in 1963, my employment had taken me many times around the world and I longed to get back to where strangers waved at you when you drove by and not with a weapon or an obscene gesture. There is just something about how country folk wave at everyone when they drive by, and I had forgotten how comforting that is. After living in the desert, where there was very little green and you could see for miles, the green and pine trees of southern Mississippi took some getting used to.

I am getting a little far from my story. Mary Simms and my mom were the co-masters of the family home. Over the years, I had lived in so many far away places and was on the move all the time that I could not visit my parents very often. When I was able to visit, it was a quick flight in one day and out the next and I never met Mary. Mary had been helping mom around the house for many years and in this time, Mary had became not only a helping hand around the house, but a day-trip traveling companion with my mom.

The day after my parents passed away, I pulled my rental car into their driveway, but I had no idea how I was going to get inside. I was getting back into my car to see if my dad's banker or attorney had a key.

Mary opened the door, greeting me, saying, "Harold, Jr., I've been wanting to meet you for so long. I knew you were coming and I've got coffee already making for you. You come on inside right now, you hear." It had been a long time since any one had called me Harold, Jr. and it was comforting. As the weeks passed, Mary stayed on with me. She and I decided that I did not need as much help around the house as my mom and we agreed that she would come over every Tuesday and Thursday to dust, straighten-up the house and do some washing and ironing.

This was in February and come the next fall, I had my first chance in many years to hunt at one of the camps that I associated with my youth. Between my dad's banker and his attorney, I got my fair share of deer that season. One week that fall, Mary came over on her usual day and asked me, "Harold, Jr., what are you going to do with all that deer meat that you got?"

"I'm not sure," I said.

"Well, let me give you a hand and we are going to cook up something real good for your dinner."

That "something" was one of the finest stews I had ever put in my mouth. I asked Mary to give me the recipe and she said, "It ain't got no recipe, Mr. Harold. You just make it." In the spirit of that moment in time, I have left Mary Simms' Stew recipe just as it was spoken to me.

Three years later, a former employee and coworker of mine called. How he tracked me down, I will never know. Somewhere in the conversation he said, "I sense that you are like an old race horse, kicking at the stall and longing to get back on the race track. Why don't you move up here and go to work for me? I need someone like you who can take the arrows for me. You might even have some fun." I took the job and I met Miss Anne.

After several dates, I invited Anne over to my home for dinner. Not sure what to cook, I thought about Mary Simms and her venison stew. I thought, "If I cook that venison stew for Anne and she likes it, I just may have to marry her." She did and I did.

Mary Simms' Venison Stew

INGREDIENTS

All-purpose flour

Salt and pepper

Paper sack

Venison stew meat, cut into
  1½- to 2-inch chunks

Bacon drippings

Potatoes, unpeeled and
  quartered

Onions, peeled and quartered

Bell pepper, sliced

Carrots, sliced

Water

Cooked brown rice, optional

1 Season flour with salt and pepper and place it in a paper sack. Drop in venison chucks and shake bag to coat the venison.

2 Heat drippings in a stockpot and brown venison on all sides.

3 Add vegetables. Pour in enough water to almost cover. Set heat to low, cover and simmer 1 hour. Add more water as sauce thickens.

4 Serve with rice if desired.

Carrot, Parsnip and Venison Stew

1½ cups water

½ cup beer

2 (1-ounce) envelopes onion gravy mix

1 tablespoon packed brown sugar

¼ teaspoon ground thyme

2½ pounds venison stew meat, cut into 1-inch chunks

3 tablespoons vegetable oil

1 bay leaf, halved

6 carrots, cut into 1-inch pieces

6 medium parsnips, cut in 1-inch cubes

1 cup fresh or frozen green peas

1 In a small mixing bowl, blend water, beer, onion gravy mix, brown sugar, and thyme and set aside.

2 In large pot or Dutch oven, brown meat in oil over medium-high heat.

3 Add beer mixture and bay leaf to pot. Reduce heat. Cover and simmer until meat is almost tender, 1 to 1½ hours; stir occasionally.

4 Add carrots and parsnips. Cover and cook 20 minutes longer.

5 Add peas, cover and cook 5 to 10 minutes.

SERVES 4 TO 6

Rich Venison Mushroom Stew

Given to the author by Richard Carmichael, Chief of the Klan of Carmichael, Carmichael Estate Farm Meats, Biggar, Scotland.

2 pounds boneless venison, cut into large chunks

2½ ounces red wine vinegar

4 bay leaves, divided

2 teaspoons salt

2 teaspoons pepper

All-purpose flour

Cooking oil

1 onion, finely chopped

2 tablespoons all-purpose flour

¾ pint beef broth

Salt and pepper to taste

½ teaspoon sugar

¾ pound small mushrooms

SERVES 4 TO 6

1 Marinate venison for 24 hours in vinegar and water to cover along with 2 bay leaves, 2 teaspoons salt and 2 teaspoons pepper.

2 Drain venison, reserving marinade. Dry meat well. Dust venison with well-seasoned flour; brown in batches in oil.

3 Transfer venison to a 4-pint (8-inch) casserole dish.

4 Sauté onion until just clear. Sprinkle with 2 tablespoons flour, pour in reserved marinade liquid and beef broth and bring to a boil while stirring.

5 Pour sauce over meat; season well with salt and pepper. Add sugar and remaining 2 bay leaves. Cover tightly and simmer over low heat until meat is tender and gravy is dark. Shoulder meat may need as little as 1 hour and 30 minutes; lesser cuts will need considerably longer. Stir occasionally.

6 When ready, remove bay leaves. If not being served the same day, refrigerate overnight. To finish the dish, bring everything to room temperature, add mushrooms, pushing well down into the gravy, and bake at 375° for 25 minutes.

Irish Stew

This is a variation of an old Irish recipe.

INGREDIENTS

1 pound sliced bacon

2 pounds venison link sausage, cut 2 inches long

2 large onions, sliced

2 cloves garlic

4 large potatoes, sliced thick

2 carrots, thickly sliced

1 large bunch of miscellaneous fresh herbs, tied with cotton string

Black pepper to taste

Apple cider or apple wine

Fresh parsley, chopped

1 Fry bacon until crisp and place in large stockpot.

2 Brown sausage in bacon drippings. Transfer sausage to stockpot.

3 Soften sliced onions and whole garlic cloves in the drippings and add to stockpot along with potatoes and carrots.

4 Bury herbs in the middle of the mixture. Sprinkle with pepper. Cover with apple cider. Cook 1½ hours over low heat; do not allow stew to boil.

5 Remove spice bundle. Garnish with chopped parsley.

SERVES 6

Quick and Easy Slow-Cooked Venison Stew and Gravy

INGREDIENTS

3 tablespoons vegetable shortening

2½ pounds venison stew meat, cut into 2-inch cubes

½ teaspoon salt

½ teaspoon pepper

1 cup water

¼ cup English peas

¼ cup diced carrots

1 tablespoon all-purpose flour

1 cup cold water

Sliced tomatoes

Cooked brown rice for 4

1 Melt shortening in a large pot. Sprinkle venison with salt and pepper. Sauté venison until it is just brown; do not overcook.

2 Add 1 cup water, cover and simmer 1 to 2 hours or until just tender. Stir in English peas and carrots the last 10 minutes. Stir occasionally to keep from sticking.

3 Mix flour into 1 cup cold water and stir into venison. Cover and simmer 15 minutes. If the gravy is too thick add a little more water.

4 Serve with sliced tomatoes and brown rice.

SERVES 4

Vegetable and Venison Stew

1½ pounds venison, cut in 2-inch cubes

6 medium potatoes, cut in chunks

6 carrots, cut in ½-inch pieces

3 celery stalks, cut in 2-inch pieces

1 (1-ounce) package onion soup mix

1 (8-ounce) can tomato sauce

1 (2-ounce) can mushroom bits and pieces

1 large clove garlic, minced

Salt and pepper to taste

1 Preheat oven to 350°. Place venison, potatoes, carrots and celery in a covered casserole dish.

2 Sprinkle with onion soup mix. Spread on tomato sauce, mushrooms and garlic. Salt and pepper to taste.

3 Cover and bake 1½ hours.

SERVES 6

Sweet and Sour Stew

2 pounds venison stew meat, 1½- to 2-inch cubes

Canola or other vegetable oil

1 large onion, cut into large pieces

1 (28-ounce) can crushed tomatoes

½ cup apple cider vinegar

½ cup packed dark brown sugar

1 green bell pepper, cut into large strips

1 In a large pot or Dutch oven, gently brown venison in oil. Do not cook.

2 Add onion and lightly brown. Add tomatoes, vinegar and brown sugar.

3 Add just enough water to keep venison and vegetables from sticking. Cover and simmer over low heat 2 to 3 hours. Add more water as may be needed.

4 Ten minutes before serving, mix in bell pepper and bring to a simmer.

SERVES 4

Pearl Onion and English Pea Stew

INGREDIENTS

2 pounds venison, cut in 2-inch cubes

½ cup all-purpose flour

4 tablespoons vegetable oil

2 teaspoons salt

½ teaspoon white pepper

1 teaspoon minced fresh rosemary

6 tablespoons dried parsley

1 tablespoon paprika

Hot water

8 to 10 pearl onions, peeled

1 cup frozen or fresh English peas

1 cup dry red wine

French bread for 4

1 Dredge venison in flour. Add the oil to a hot skillet and just brown venison on all sides.

2 Add spices and enough hot water to cover. Simmer over very low heat 1 hour. Allow liquid to reduce to a thin sauce.

3 Add pearl onions, English peas and wine; simmer 30 minutes more.

4 Serve with sliced and lightly toasted French bread.

SERVES 4

There are very few liars at deer camp

Salt Pork, Venison and Vegetable Stew

INGREDIENTS

4 tablespoons cooking oil

½ pound salt pork, cut in
   ½-inch pieces

2 pounds venison steak, cut in
   2-inch pieces

4 tablespoons all-purpose flour

6 cups canned beef broth

1 large tomato, chopped

2 medium carrots, sliced

2 medium stalks celery, sliced

2 medium potatoes, cut in
   1-inch pieces

12 small onions

1 tablespoon chopped fresh
   parsley

Salt and pepper to taste

1 cup fresh or frozen English
   peas

1 Heat oil in a large saucepan and sauté salt pork until lightly browned. Remove and set aside.

2 Brown venison over high heat in 4 tablespoons salt pork drippings.

3 Sift in flour; lower heat and brown for 2 to 3 minutes. Place in a slow cooker; add beef broth and cook on low heat 8 hours. Add more liquid if necessary.

4 Add all other ingredients, except peas, and continue to simmer until stew thickens.

5 Simmer peas in a separate pan until just tender. Drain peas and spoon over stew when served.

SERVES 6

SOUPS, STEWS & CHILIS

Crockpot Barbecue Stew

INGREDIENTS

3 pounds venison, cut in 2-inch pieces

1 cup diced yellow onion

4 cloves garlic, chopped

1 cup apple cider vinegar

½ cup Worcestershire sauce

2 teaspoons Lawrey's Natural Choice Seasoning for meat

1½ teaspoons Seasoned Salt for Wild Game (page 204) or other seasoned salt

1 pound smoked bacon slices

2 cups ketchup

½ cup sorghum molasses or other dark syrup

½ cup packed dark brown sugar

1 Place venison, onion, garlic, vinegar, Worcestershire and both seasonings in slow cooker. Cook on high 1 to 2 hours until meat is cooked.

2 Fry smoked bacon crisp and crumble. Add bacon, ketchup, molasses and brown sugar to slow cooker. Turn to low and cook 6 hours more.

SERVES 4

Seasoned Salt for Wild Game

This is an outstanding seasoning for most wild game and fowl. Juniper berries add a little English flavoring to the seasoning. Juniper berries are the flavoring used in gin.

INGREDIENTS

1 teaspoon nutmeg

3 teaspoons ground juniper berries

2 teaspoons black pepper

2 teaspoons ground red pepper

2 teaspoons oregano

2 teaspoons garlic powder

2 teaspoons onion powder

2 teaspoons celery salt

2 teaspoons mustard powder

2 teaspoons ground thyme

2 teaspoons ground savory

2 teaspoons curry powder

½ to 1 cup salt to taste

1 Mix all ingredients, except salt.

2 Start by adding ½ cup salt. Taste and add salt until you are satisfied.

CHILIS

In my opinion, I do not think that there has ever been or will ever be a deer camp that does not serve venison chili at least twice each year—sometimes more. If there is one, I am not sure that I will wish to spend much time there. I like chili that is hot as Hades. I like chili that is mild. I like chili with ground venison and I like chili with chunks of meat.

I accuse my granddad of "causing" me to love chili the way that I do, and I accuse my mom for giving me her cast-iron stomach and my love of spicy food. My grandfather was the consummate maker of fine chili. I remember sitting in his kitchen on a cold Saturday morning and watching him assemble all of his ingredients like a chemist formulating a new miracle drug. He would debone a deer hindquarter, separate the muscle groups, twice fine-grind all the red meat and use half for his chili—I don't remember what he did with the other half.

He would orchestrate the sautéing of his onions and the browning of his ground venison just as if he were conducting a symphony in the greatest concert hall in the world. I can still see him twirling his wooden stirring spoon to Hank Williams and Earnest Tubbs as the music blared from the wooden console radio sitting next door in his living room. This was an all-day cooking affair. When everything was safety tucked away in that big black and ancient cast-iron cooking pot and the stove was set on a low simmer, he and I would go for a walk to feed the chickens and check on the cows. For the rest of the day, it would be one round trip after another. First we would stir the chili and then walk to the barn, then return to stir the chili and walk to the hen house, then back to stir the chili and then out to change the oil in his tractor. Around 4:00 in the afternoon, he would make his final stir, remove the pot from the stove and allow it to rest in the refrigerator until supper time—granddad called it "mellowing." I can tell you one thing, if it had mellowed any more, it would have been too good to eat. My taste buds have aged a bit over the years and my digestive system is no longer as tolerant of spicy food as it once was. But, I still enjoy chili.

SOUPS, STEWS & CHILIS

Hell-Fire Venison Chili

If this chili is not hot enough for you, add more Tabasco sauce and red pepper flakes.

INGREDIENTS

4 tablespoons cooking oil

2 pounds ground venison

2 pounds ground beef

8 ounces Worcestershire sauce

½ tablespoon oregano

2 tablespoons garlic salt

1 tablespoon seasoned salt

80 ounces tomato sauce

6 ounces garlic, minced

8 ounces hot green chiles, chopped

20 fresh jalapeños peppers, chopped, with seeds

8 ounces Datil Hellish Relish or other hot relish

4 (15-ounce) cans kidney beans

1 (15-ounce) can pinto beans

3 teaspoons Tabasco sauce or more to taste

⅛ teaspoon red pepper flakes

5 large onions, minced

8 ounces Mexican-style hot relish

1 Heat cooking oil in a large skillet. Mix venison, beef, Worcestershire sauce, oregano, garlic salt and seasoned salt and brown the meats.

2 In a large stockpot, mix remaining ingredients. Heat on medium high until near boiling.

3 Transfer browned meat and cooking liquid into stockpot. Cover and simmer on very low heat 6 to 8 hours. Stir frequently to keep from sticking.

SERVES 10

Jalapeño and Beer Crockpot Chili

3 medium onions, chopped

2 medium green bell peppers, chopped

2 stalks celery, sliced

2 cloves garlic, minced

1 fresh jalapeño pepper, seeded and diced

8 pounds venison, coarsely ground

7 ounces green chiles, diced

1 (28-ounce) can stewed tomatoes, quartered

1 (15-ounce) can tomato sauce

1 (6-ounce) can tomato paste

6 ounces chili powder

2 tablespoons ground cumin

Tabasco sauce to taste

12 ounces beer

3 bay leaves

Garlic powder to taste

Salt and pepper to taste

12 ounces more or less water

Flour tortillas for 16 to 20

1 Place all ingredients except tortillas into a slow cooker and cook over low heat 8 to 10 hours. Remove bay leaves.

2 Refrigerate overnight.

3 Reheat and serve with warmed flour tortillas.

SERVES 16 TO 20

Cornmeal-Crusted Black Bean Chili

INGREDIENTS

2 tablespoons olive oil

1 pound ground venison

½ cup sliced fresh mushrooms

1 cup minced onion

½ cup diced green bell pepper

2 cloves garlic, minced

½ cup diced red bell pepper

2 jalapeño peppers, seeded and minced

1 (14-ounce) can beef broth

2 (15-ounce) cans black beans

1 (28-ounce) can whole Roma tomatoes, quartered

2 cups water, divided

1½ tablespoons chili powder

1 teaspoon ground oregano

1 bay leaf

Ground red pepper to taste

Salt to taste

2 (8.5-ounce) packages Jiffy Corn Muffin Mix, plus ingredients to prepare

1 Heat olive oil in a large ovenproof pot or Dutch oven over medium heat; add and venison and mushrooms and cook until venison is browned.

2 Add onion and green bell peppers and sauté until onion is just clear.

3 Add garlic, red bell pepper and jalapeños and sauté for just a few moments.

4 Add beef broth and scrape the bits from bottom of the pot.

5 Add beans, tomatoes, 1½ cups water and spices. Remove from heat. Remove bay leaf.

6 Preheat oven to 350º. Prepare corn muffin mix according to package directions but do not bake. Dilute ⅓ cup corn muffin mix with remaining ½ cup water. Stir into chili broth.

7 Spoon on remaining prepared corn muffin mix so that it floats on top of the chili. Cover pot and bake 20 to 40 minutes or until cornbread is slightly browned and crusty.

SERVES 4 TO 6

Chunky Venison and Red Kidney Bean Chili

4 tablespoons canola oil, divided

1 green bell pepper, chopped

2 onions, chopped fine

2 cloves garlic, crushed

1 pound venison, cut in chunks

1 (8-ounce) can tomatoes

1 cup canned beef broth

4 tablespoons tomato paste

1 tablespoon mild chili powder

2 bay leaves

1 teaspoon oregano

¼ teaspoon red pepper

1 teaspoon ground cumin

2 (4-ounce) cans chopped chiles

2 tablespoons packed brown sugar

Salt and pepper to taste

1 (14-ounce) can red kidney beans

Cooked rice for 4 to 6

Crackers

Shredded Cheddar cheese

1 Heat 2 tablespoons oil in a skillet and sauté bell pepper, onions and garlic until soft. Remove vegetables to a large pot or Dutch oven.

2 Heat remaining 2 tablespoons oil in a skillet and gently brown the venison. Transfer venison to the pot with vegetables.

3 Stir in tomatoes, broth, tomato paste, chili powder, bay leaves, oregano, red pepper, cumin, chopped chiles, brown sugar, salt and pepper. Simmer over low heat 3 to 4 hours. If using a slow cooker, simmer on a low setting 6 to 8 hours.

4 Add kidney beans and simmer another 30 minutes. Remove bay leaves. Season with additional salt and pepper, if needed.

5 Serve over cooked rice with crackers and shredded Cheddar cheese.

SERVES 4 TO 6

Southern-Style Chili con Carne

2 pounds venison, cut in 1-inch cubes

2 tablespoons olive oil, divided

2 large onions, sliced

10 cloves garlic, minced

1 quart canned beef broth

4 tablespoons chili powder

1 tablespoon ground cumin

2 tablespoons paprika

1 teaspoon cayenne pepper

2 tablespoons crushed dried oregano

¾ teaspoon salt

¼ cup fine yellow cornmeal

Water

Cornbread for 4 to 6

Coleslaw for 4 to 6

1 In small batches, brown venison in 1 tablespoon olive oil and set aside.

2 In a 4-quart pot or Dutch oven, heat remaining 1 tablespoon olive oil and sauté onions until just clear. Add garlic and sauté for just a minute.

3 Add broth and remaining spices. Bring to a boil, reduce to a simmer, cover and simmer at least 3 hours or until venison is tender. Place in refrigerator overnight.

4 The next day, remove hardened fat. To serve, reheat.

5 Thicken by mixing cornmeal with no more than 1 cup water to make a thin paste. Add this quickly to the chili as it simmers, stirring quickly and briskly.

6 Serve in bowls with cornbread and coleslaw on the side.

SERVES 4 TO 6

Chili con Queso

1 pound ground venison

2 tablespoons butter

1 (28-ounce) can crushed
   tomatoes

1 hot chile pepper, chopped

1 small onion, chopped

Salt and pepper to taste

1 pound Velveeta cheese

Tortilla chips

1 Brown venison in butter and drain.

2 Place venison, tomatoes, chile pepper
   and onion in a slow cooker. Season to
   taste with salt and pepper. Cook on low
   6 to 8 hours.

3 Melt cheese. Serve chili in individual
   bowls with melted cheese on top and
   tortilla chips on the side.

SERVES 2 TO 4

Italian-Style Sausage Chili

INGREDIENTS

2 pounds venison link sausage, casings removed

3 tablespoons corn oil

½ teaspoon Old Bay Seasoning or other similar seasoning

1 small onion, chopped

1 green bell pepper, chopped fine

1½ tablespoons chili powder

2 (15-ounce) cans Italian-style tomatoes

1 (6-ounce) can tomato paste

½ teaspoon garlic powder

1 teaspoon pepper

½ cup water

1 (16-ounce) can kidney beans, drained

1 fresh jalapeño pepper, seeded and chopped

Hot sauce to taste

1 (12-ounce) can beer

Tortilla chips

Shredded sharp Cheddar cheese

1 Dice or slice sausage, and sprinkle with Old Bay Seasoning.

2 Heat oil in a large skillet. Brown the sausage in the oil.

3 Pour off drippings and add onion, bell pepper, chili powder, tomatoes, tomato paste, garlic powder, pepper and water. Cook over low heat 30 minutes, stirring occasionally.

4 Add kidney beans, jalapeño and hot sauce to taste. Cover and simmer another 30 minutes.

5 Just before serving stir in the beer. Serve with tortilla chips and a little shredded sharp Cheddar sprinkled on top.

SERVES 4 TO 6

Next Day Venison Chili

2 pounds course-ground
venison

2 large cloves garlic, minced

1 teaspoon paprika

2 tablespoons chili powder

1 tablespoon salt

1 tablespoon white pepper

1 tablespoon hot chile pods,
diced

1 quart water, more or less

Shredded sharp Cheddar
cheese

Green onion stems, finely
chopped

Saltine crackers or Fritos

1 Brown venison to rare in a large skillet with a little oil. Transfer venison and drippings into a slow cooker or large cooking pot.

2 Add the spices with just enough water to cover meat. Cook over very low heat 4 to 5 hours. Stir to keep venison from sticking. Add additional water as needed.

3 Refrigerate overnight. Reheat and serve the next day in individual bowls topped with cheese, green onions and crumbled crackers or Fritos.

SERVES 6 TO 8

Fresh Leaf Lettuce—12 Months of the Year

I was once a meat and potatoes person. When I retired and purchased our little home in the woods, one of the first things I did was put in a small vegetable garden. I don't remember why I did it, but I designated a small portion of the garden for a fresh lettuce bed. I didn't have a clue about how to grow lettuce or what species to plant.

Sometimes ignorance is a blessing. I saw several different packages of mixed leaf lettuce seeds at my local nursery and I just sprinkled the seeds around. Where I grew up, the country folks planted only a single spring-summer garden and this was my intent with my lettuce bed. By August, some of the less heat tolerant species had died, but others were still thriving. Again ignorance was a blessing. I left the lettuce bed alone and continued to harvest fresh lettuce throughout the winter.

What did I learn? I learned that lettuce, like spinach, thrives in cool weather. I now plant my lettuce bed twice a year (April and August) and I have fresh-picked lettuce for dinner 12 months out of the year. I also learned something else about harvesting my lettuce. If I pluck the whole plant, the plant is gone. However, if I pluck only the bottom leaves and leave a small crown of leaves, the lettuce plant will continue to grow upward and I will have a long growing season.

At deer camp, we frequently have leftover roast or other venison from the previous evening. Incorporating thin-sliced leftover venison with a

fresh salad is a fine way to add an agreeable change-of-pace to the same old lettuce and Italian salad dressing salads. If we are to go to the trouble to make a salad—why not go ahead and make it an interesting salad?

Doe Tracks and Missing Lettuce

I am normally a very sharing person and I do not even mind sharing an occasional meal from my lettuce bed with the local critters. However, when I am visited night after night—enough of this sharing. After four days of being visited by this young doe, it became apparent to me that she had found a handy place to dine and, after a few more nights, I would no longer have a lettuce bed. I called the game warden to see if I could be issued a Special Predator Permit. He came out that day to investigate the "crime scene." Since I did not have sufficient

"commercial crop damage" to justify a predator permit, he did suggest an alternative which was to install an electric fence around my garden. For some unknown reason, after his visit the doe left me alone and I did not install the electric fence.

Basic Bubba and Bubbaleen Venison Salad

INGREDIENTS

3 heads lettuce, torn into pieces

12 tomatoes, quartered

9 stalks green onions, chopped

30 green or black olives, chopped

1 whole venison loin, roasted and sliced thin

¾ cup herb-flavored croutons, optional

3 (8-ounce) bottles salad dressing of choice

1 Mix all ingredients together in a large bowl and serve.

SERVES 20

Fajita Venison Salad

INGREDIENTS

1 red bell pepper, sliced thin

1 green bell pepper, sliced thin

1 onion, sliced thin

3 tablespoons Cajun Spice Mix or other Creole-type seasoning

Canola, olive or other oil

1 pound venison, cut into strips

2 tablespoons sweet chili sauce

Boston or other lettuce

1 avocado, sliced long ways

8 fried or steamed corn or wheat tortillas, cut into strips

8 cherry tomatoes, halved

Sour cream

CAJUN SPICE MIX:

1 tablespoon paprika

2 teaspoons oregano

½ teaspoon rosemary

1 tablespoon cumin

1 teaspoon chili powder

2 teaspoons garlic powder

1 teaspoon packed brown sugar

1 teaspoon salt

1 teaspoon black pepper

1 Mix bell peppers and onion with Cajun Spice Mix.

2 Preheat a heavy pan with a little oil and sauté peppers and onion until they begin to soften.

3 Add venison and brown. Cook to no more than rare to medium rare. Stir in chili sauce.

4 Line each serving plate with Boston lettuce. Spoon venison-salad mixture on top. Garnish with avocado, tortilla strips, tomatoes and sour cream.

CAJUN SPICE MIX:

5 Mix all ingredients together and use for a real Cajun flavor.

SERVES 4

Pasta and Venison Salad
with Spring Vegetables

OLIVE BASIL DRESSING:

2 tablespoons olive oil

1 teaspoon minced garlic

3 tablespoons minced green
olives

¼ cup chopped fresh basil

Salt and pepper to taste

SALAD:

3 tablespoons olive oil, divided

1 pound venison loin

½ pound mushrooms,
quartered

3 tomatoes, quartered

1 zucchini, cut ribbon-thin
lengthwise

Cooked pasta for 4

Sprigs fresh basil

OLIVE BASIL DRESSING:

1 Make dressing by combining 2
tablespoons olive oil, garlic, olives, basil
and salt and pepper. Set aside.

TO PREPARE SALAD:

2 Preheat oven to 425°. Heat 1 tablespoon
olive oil in a large skillet and brown
venison on all sides. Transfer venison
to a roasting dish and insert a meat
thermometer into one end. Bake to 140°
on thermometer, no more than rare to
medium rare. Remove from oven, cover
with aluminum foil and let rest 10
minutes.

3 Heat remaining 2 tablespoons olive oil
in a skillet and cook mushrooms 2 to
3 minutes. Add tomatoes and zucchini
and cook another 2 to 3 minutes.

4 Gently combine pasta and vegetables
with dressing.

5 Slice venison across the grain into
¼-inch-thin slices and fan in middle of
serving plates. Arrange pasta around
venison. Garnish with a sprig of fresh
basil.

SERVES 4

Caesar-Style Venison Salad

CAESAR SALAD DRESSING:

1 clove garlic, peeled and sliced

½ cup plus 2 tablespoons olive oil, divided

1 cup cubed French bread

2 heads Romaine lettuce

1½ teaspoons salt

¼ teaspoon dry mustard

1/8 teaspoon pepper

5 anchovy fillets, ground to paste

⅛ teaspoon Worcestershire sauce

3 tablespoons red wine vinegar

1 egg

Juice of 1 lemon

3 tablespoons grated Parmesan cheese

SALAD:

4 venison loin steaks, cut 1½-inches thick

1 tablespoon canola or other oil

Salt and pepper to taste

Crisp lettuce, cut in 2-inch pieces

Parmesan cheese to taste

Anchovies, croutons, and sliced stuffed olives to taste

CAESAR SALAD DRESSING:

1 Add garlic to ½ cup olive oil and refrigerate 24 hours.

2 Sauté bread cubes in 2 tablespoons olive oil and set aside.

3 Break lettuce into 2-inch lengths and wash in very cold water. Shake well and allow to drain.

4 Bring garlic-infused oil to room temperature, discard garlic slices and mix with remaining ingredients.

TO PREPARE SALAD:

5 Cook venison steaks to rare in oil and season with salt and pepper. Allow to rest 10 minutes and cut across the grain into thin slices or slivers.

6 Place all ingredients into a large salad bowl. Add Caesar Salad Dressing to taste and mix well. Serve at room temperature.

SERVES 4

VEGETABLES

When thinking about vegetable dishes that go well with venison at deer camp, I am reminded of my father. Dad could never sit down and enjoy a meal without having his bread, butter, and iced tea sitting on the table. Depending on whatever part of the world you are in, there are always particular culinary items that every culture associates with a meal. Whether it is vegetables that are cooked in with my venison or vegetables that serve as a side dish, I must have my vegetables or it is just not a proper venison meal.

Since I have small summer and winter vegetable gardens, it is only natural that what I grow will go with most of the wild game, fowl, and fish I harvest. My gardens grow nothing that is exotic. One might think my herb garden is exotic, but for my purpose, rosemary, thyme, basil, oregano, savory, cilantro, marjoram, ginger, garlic and onion chives are exactly what I need to make my meals complete.

Since my vegetable beds are small, I decided early on that I cannot grow all the vegetables I enjoy in one growing season or even in one year. Instead of attempting to grow a small amount of all the vegetables, I grow a large amount of a few items. By doing this, I am able to grow and freeze a two-year supply at one time and then grow different vegetables the next time around. One summer I might grow corn, bush beans, peppers (cayenne and jalapeño), zucchini squash, tomatoes (large and cherry) and eggplant. The next summer and in the same beds, I might grow pole beans, okra, yellow squash, Roma tomatoes, ginger, green bell peppers and cucumbers.

One fall I might grow turnips for greens and the next fall turnips for roots. One fall I might grow broccoli, Brussels sprouts, carrots and spinach. The next fall, in the same beds, I might grow cauliflower, cabbage, beets and onions. This is in addition to my twice a year planting of leaf lettuce, radishes, green onions and leeks.

If you have never had the opportunity to enjoy vegetables that are fresh-picked from your garden and cooked that day, I can promise you they do not taste anything like the six-day- or two-week-old, out-of-season vegetables that are grown south of the equator and flown to northern markets—there is just no comparison. Young and tender fresh vegetables require very little cooking.

I cannot imagine eating breakfast without coffee, I am unable to enjoy a hot cobbler without a scoop of vanilla ice cream and eating a venison main dish at deer camp, without my vegetables, is something I am unwilling to do.

A note about vegetable recipes:

- Recipes for 10 or less should not be halved. But to serve a large number of people, all of the vegetable recipes in this section can be doubled.

- Recipes for 12 or more can be halved. To serve a large number of people, all of the vegetable recipes in this section can be doubled.

Miss Anne's Tuna, English Pea and Macaroni & Cheese Casserole

If I have an all-time, number one most favorite dish of Miss Anne's, then this is it. Since she knows how much I like it and my predisposition to eat the whole casserole at one sitting, she won't cook it for me very often.

INGREDIENTS

- 1 (5.5-ounce) package Kraft macaroni and cheese, plus ingredients to prepare
- 1 (5-ounce) can tuna, drained
- ½ small onion, diced
- ½ (15-ounce) can sweet English peas
- 1 (10.75-ounce) can cream of mushroom soup

1 Preheat oven to 350°. Cook macaroni and cheese according to package directions.

2 Mix in tuna, onion, peas and mushroom soup and pour into a casserole dish. Bake 30 to 45 minutes. When about half done, stir once.

SERVES 4

Ten-Minute Cauliflower and Instant Rice Pilaf

INGREDIENTS

1 tablespoon olive or other cooking oil

4 cups chopped cauliflower

½ teaspoon salt

¾ cup chicken broth

1 teaspoon grated orange zest

¼ cup orange juice

¼ cup raisins

⅔ cup instant or minute rice

½ cup sliced green onions

1 Heat oil in a large saucepan over medium heat. Add cauliflower and salt; cook, stirring, until softened.

2 Add chicken broth, orange zest, orange juice and raisins. Bring to a boil over high heat.

3 Stir in instant rice and green onions. Remove from heat, cover and let stand until liquid is absorbed, about 5 minutes. Fluff with fork and serve.

SERVES 4

Easy Baked Cream-Style Corn

INGREDIENTS

1½ cups butter or margarine, melted

1½ pounds saltine or Ritz Crackers, coarsely crumbled, divided

1 tablespoon pepper

3 gallons cream-style corn, divided

3 pounds grated Cheddar cheese

2 quarts milk

1 Preheat oven to 325°. Mix butter, crackers and pepper. Pour half the corn into greased 18x24-inch disposable aluminum roasting pan.

2 Cover with half the cracker mixture. Spread with Cheddar cheese. Pour over remaining corn.

3 Cover with remaining cracker mixture. Pour milk evenly over top. Bake 45 minutes or until browned and bubbling.

SERVES 100

Skillet-Fried Corn

2 slices smoked bacon

2 teaspoons cooking oil or bacon or sausage drippings

3 cups cut fresh corn kernels (about 4 ears) or 3 cups frozen

¼ teaspoon pepper

⅔ cup milk or more if needed

1 Fry bacon until crisp; drain.

2 Cook corn and pepper in hot skillet until corn begins to brown. Add milk and bring to a simmer. Scrape pan to remove any bits. Reduce heat to medium and simmer 5 minutes or until most of the milk has evaporated. If milk evaporates before corn is tender, add more milk a tablespoon at a time.

3 Crumble bacon and stir into corn.

SERVES 4

Easy Baked Tamale-Style Corn

2 eggs

2 (4-ounce) cans chopped mild green chiles

¾ cup yellow cornmeal

2 (15-ounce) cans whole-kernel corn, drained

¾ teaspoon garlic salt

½ teaspoon baking powder

6 tablespoons corn oil

½ pound grated Cheddar cheese

1 Preheat oven to 350°. Beat eggs.

2 Mix remaining ingredients and stir into eggs. Pour into a lightly greased 1½-quart casserole and bake 1 hour.

SERVES 12

Italian-Style Oven-Roasted Asparagus Spears

2 pounds asparagus stalks

1 tablespoon olive oil or other vegetable oil

1 tablespoon white wine

1 tablespoon balsamic, rice wine or other mild vinegar

3 garlic cloves, minced

Salt and pepper to taste

¼ teaspoon rosemary flakes

¼ teaspoon marjoram flakes

¼ teaspoon bay leaf flakes

¼ teaspoon thyme flakes

¼ cup or more grated Parmesan cheese

Lemon wedges

1 Wash and cut off tough ends of asparagus and spread out on a shallow baking pan.

2 Make a marinade by combining olive oil, wine, balsamic vinegar, garlic and spices. Pour marinade over asparagus, cover with plastic wrap and marinate 2 to 3 hours.

3 Preheat oven to 400°. Drain and discard marinade. When ready to bake, sprinkle Parmesan cheese over top of asparagus. Depending on thickness of asparagus stalks, bake 8 to 10 minutes or until lightly browned. Serve on a platter with lemon wedges.

SERVES 4

Mashed Turnips and Bacon Bits

I associate deer hunting season with the harvesting of my fall turnip crop. Since turnips have a long shelf life and they require no refrigeration, I carry a sack of my turnips along with me to deer camp and we enjoy an occasional turnip meal—until the sack is empty.

INGREDIENTS

2 pounds turnips

2 tablespoons butter, room temperature

Pinch salt

Pinch pepper

Pinch garlic powder

½ pound bacon

1 Peel and cube turnips. Place in a small pot of lightly salted water and boil until turnips are fork-tender. Drain and mash or press though a potato ricer.

2 Mix in butter, salt, pepper and garlic powder.

3 Fry bacon crisp, drain on paper towels and crumble.

4 Pour off all but 3 tablespoons of bacon drippings. In the same skillet, heat and mix turnips and bacon bits in bacon drippings.

SERVES 4

Tex-Mex Jalapeño Hash Brown Potatoes

1½ pounds potatoes

3 tablespoons cooking oil, divided

1 large onion, cut in ½-inch chunks

¾ teaspoon salt

¼ teaspoon pepper

½ teaspoon cumin

1 green bell pepper, cut in ½-inch chunks

1 red bell pepper, cut in ½-inch chunks

2 pickled jalapeño peppers, minced

1 tablespoon minced cilantro

1 Cook potatoes in boiling water 25 minutes or until just tender. Drain. When cool enough to handle, peel and cut in ½-inch chunks.

2 Heat 2 tablespoons oil in a skillet. Add onion, potatoes, salt, pepper and cumin. Cook, stirring frequently, 10 minutes or until onion is golden brown.

3 Add remaining 1 tablespoon oil and peppers. Cover and cook 10 minutes, stirring frequently, or until peppers are tender.

4 Remove cover and cook 5 minutes more until potatoes are golden brown and crusty on edges. Sprinkle with cilantro.

SERVES 4

Creamed-Style New Potatoes and Green Peas

INGREDIENTS

1 pound small red new potatoes

1 (10-ounce) package frozen green peas

3 tablespoons chopped white or yellow onion

2 tablespoons butter

2 tablespoons all-purpose flour

¼ teaspoon salt

⅛ teaspoon pepper

½ teaspoon dry or 1 teaspoon chopped fresh dill weed

1½ cups whole milk

1 Cook unpeeled potatoes in boiling water 20 minutes or until fork-tender. Drain and set aside.

2 Sauté peas and onion in butter until onion is just clear.

3 Mix in flour, salt, pepper and dill. Stir flour mixture into milk and heat in a small cooking pot until mixture boils and begins to thicken; stir often.

4 Add potatoes, stir and heat.

SERVES 4

How to Bake a Potato

Any size and any type of potato can be baked. But, it is the large brown russet potato that we normally think of when we refer to a "baked potato."

PREPARING TO BAKE THE BIG BROWN RUSSET:

1 About an hour or so before you are ready to eat, adjust the rack to the middle of the oven, wash the potatoes under cold water and preheat the oven. Pierce each potato deeply with a fork four times along each side. Piercing is important because I have on occasion seen the steam inside an unpierced potato cause it to explode in the oven.

2 Wrapping potatoes in aluminum foil will give you soft skins; unwrapped potatoes will give you crunchy skins. The choice is yours—the cooking time is the same.

HOW HOT AND FOR HOW LONG?

3 As a general rule of thumb, in a properly preheated oven, it takes this amount of time at this temperature to bake an average size russet potato.
- 45 minutes at 400°
- 60 minutes at 350°
- 90 minutes at 325°

CHECK FOR DONENESS:

4 To see if your baked potatoes are done, stick a meat thermometer inside the largest potato. If the thermometer reads 210° or a little more, your potatoes are done. Lacking a meat thermometer, if you can easily insert a fork into the center or if the potato is soft when you squeeze it in the middle, it is done.

Warm Potato Salad

10 medium potatoes

1¾ cups vegetable, chicken or beef broth

¼ cup apple cider vinegar

¼ cup all-purpose flour

3 tablespoons sugar

½ teaspoon celery seed

⅛ teaspoon pepper

½ cup chopped white or yellow onion

3 tablespoons chopped fresh parsley

1 Place potatoes in a small pot, cover with water and heat to a boil. Reduce heat to low and cook 20 minutes or until are fork-tender. Drain, and when cool, cut into ½- to ¾-inch chunks.

2 In a small pot, mix remaining ingredients except parsley. Simmer over medium heat until mixture begins to thicken. Reduce heat and cook 5 minutes or until onion turns clear.

3 Place potatoes in a large bowl. Stir in parsley and warm dressing. Allow to stand 10 minutes before serving.

SERVES 12

Mashed Sweet Potatoes

INGREDIENTS

6 pounds sweet potatoes, peeled and cut into chunks

5 tablespoons butter

3½ tablespoons soy or teriyaki sauce

2 green onions, sliced thin

1 In 5- to 6-quart pot, place potatoes chunks and enough water to cover. Heat to boiling and then reduce heat to medium-low. Cook 10 to 15 minutes or until potato pieces are fork-tender.

2 Remove potatoes and drain water from pot. Melt butter in same pot, add potatoes and soy sauce. Mash potatoes until smooth.

3 Top with sliced green onions.

SERVES 12

Orange Glazed Sweet Potatoes

20 (40-ounce) cans sweet potatoes, drained, 2 quarts liquid reserved

2 oranges, unpeeled and sliced thin

1 pound butter or margarine, melted

1 cup cornstarch

2¼ tablespoons salt

5 pounds light brown sugar

1 Preheat oven to 375°. Grease a large roasting pan or disposable aluminum roasting pan and arrange sweet potatoes in single layer.

2 Lay on orange slices. Pour over with melted butter.

3 In a large pot, mix cornstarch, salt and brown sugar. Stir in the reserved liquid from sweet potatoes. Bring to a boil, reduce heat to a high simmer and cook 5 minutes.

4 Pour syrup over sweet potatoes and bake 20 minutes.

SERVES 100

Molasses-Glazed Carrots

INGREDIENTS

3 pounds frozen baby carrots

1 cup molasses or syrup, room temperature

1 cup butter, room temperature

3 tablespoons dark brown sugar

1 teaspoon nutmeg

1½ teaspoons cinnamon

⅓ cup inexpensive bourbon

1 Boil carrots until fork-tender, about 15 minutes; drain.

2 In a saucepan, mix together molasses, butter and brown sugar. Simmer until mixture begins to boil.

3 Add carrots, nutmeg and cinnamon. Cook and stir until carrots are glazed, 3 to 5 minutes.

4 Warm bourbon in a saucepan, ignite and pour over carrots. Shake pan until alcohol burns off.

SERVES 12

Sauerkraut, Bacon and Apples

INGREDIENTS

2¼ gallons canned sauerkraut, undrained

3 cups chopped thin-sliced bacon

3 pound onions, chopped

4 apples, pared, cored and chopped

3 tablespoons caraway seed

1 cup packed light brown sugar

1 Combine all ingredients in a large stockpot and simmer 1½ hours. Stir occasionally.

SERVES 100

Beets in Orange-Lemon Sauce

INGREDIENTS

2 (16-ounce) jars small whole beets

3 tablespoons cornstarch

2 teaspoons grated orange rind

⅔ cup orange juice

6 tablespoons lemon juice

½ cup sugar

½ cup butter

1 Drain beets and save ½ cup liquid.

2 Dissolve cornstarch in beet liquid. Mix in orange rind, orange juice, lemon juice and sugar. Simmer until sauce becomes slightly thickened and clear.

3 Stir in beets and butter and heat until beets are warm.

SERVES 12

Baked Broccoli, Mushroom and Noodle Casserole

INGREDIENTS

- 1 (16-ounce) package wide flat egg noodles
- 2 tablespoons butter or margarine
- 3 cloves garlic, minced
- 2 cups chopped onions
- 1 pound mushrooms, coarsely chopped
- 1 large bunch fresh broccoli, chopped
- ½ teaspoon salt
- Pepper to taste
- ¼ cup inexpensive dry white wine
- 3 eggs
- 1 cup sour cream
- 3 cups small-curd cottage cheese
- 1½ cups fine unseasoned breadcrumbs, divided
- 1 cup grated Cheddar cheese

1 Preheat oven to 350°. Grease a 9x13-inch baking pan or disposable aluminum baking pan.

2 Cook noodles in boiling water until about half done. Drain and rinse under cold water. Drain again and set aside.

3 Melt butter in large skillet and stir in garlic and onions. Sauté over medium heat 5 minutes or until onions begin to clear.

4 Stir in mushrooms, broccoli, salt and pepper. Cook until broccoli is bright green and just fork-tender. Remove from heat and mix in wine.

5 In large bowl, beat eggs. Mix in sour cream and cottage cheese. Add noodles, sautéed vegetables and 1 cup breadcrumbs. Mix well.

6 Spread mixture into lightly greased baking pan and top with remaining breadcrumbs and cheese. Cover and bake 30 minutes. Uncover and bake another 15 minutes.

SERVES 12

Vegetable Casserole

Can be made ahead of time and reheated in the oven.

13 pounds zucchini squash, cut into ¼-inch slices

⅓ cup plus 3 tablespoons olive or vegetable cooking olive oil

13 pounds eggplant, cut into cubes

1½ cups water

¼ cup Italian herb seasoning

1 gallon plus 9 cups canned peeled tomatoes, drained and chopped

Salt and pepper to taste

6¾ pounds grated Ricotta cheese

3 cups grated Parmesan cheese

13 eggs, beaten

1½ cups chopped parsley

6¼ cups seasoned breadcrumbs

1 Preheat oven to 350°. Steam zucchini 2 minutes or boil until almost tender. Drain on paper towels.

2 Heat oil in heavy skillet or Dutch oven over medium-high heat. Sauté eggplant 2 minutes, stirring occasionally. Add water, cover and cook 3 to 4 minutes until almost tender.

3 Stir in Italian seasoning, tomatoes and salt and pepper to taste. Cover and simmer 5 minutes.

4 Combine remaining ingredients, except breadcrumbs, in a mixing bowl.

5 Arrange half the zucchini slices in bottom of an oiled large disposable aluminum baking pan. Top with half the cheese mixture. Add a layer of half the eggplant mixture.

6 Repeat layers with remaining zucchini, cheese and eggplant. Sprinkle with breadcrumbs and bake 35 minutes.

SERVES 50

Twenty-Five Minute Green Bean Casserole

INGREDIENTS

1 (10.75-ounce) can condensed cream of mushroom soup

½ cup milk

1 teaspoon soy or teriyaki sauce

Pinch pepper

2 (16-ounce) cans green beans

1⅓ cups prepared fried onion rings, divided

1 Preheat oven to 350°. Mix mushroom soup, milk, soy sauce, pepper, beans and ⅔ cup onion rings. Pour into an ovenproof casserole dish.

2 Bake 25 minutes or until hot. Sprinkle top with remaining onion rings.

SERVES 6

Green Beans with Pecan Topping

INGREDIENTS

12 pounds frozen green beans

3 teaspoons salt

1 tablespoon pepper

1½ cups butter

1 pound pecan pieces, chopped

1 Boil green beans in salted water until fork-tender. Drain and place in a large serving dish or disposable aluminum pan. Season with salt and pepper.

2 Melt butter and add pecans and simmer 5 minutes. Pour over beans and mix well.

SERVES 50

Day-Before Baked Beans

This recipe can be made 2 to 3 days in advance and refrigerated.

2 pounds dried navy beans, soaked overnight in cold water

¾ cup molasses or sorghum syrup

1 tablespoon soy or teriyaki sauce

1 teaspoon Worcestershire sauce

¾ cup light brown sugar

1½ teaspoons salt

¼ teaspoon dry mustard

1 onion, coarsely chopped

1 clove garlic, minced

½ pound smoked bacon, in 1 piece or thick-cut

1 Preheat oven to 300°. Drain beans and place in large ovenproof casserole dish or pot. Add water to cover by ½ inch. Cover and simmer 30 minutes.

2 Stir in molasses, soy sauce, Worcestershire, brown sugar, salt, mustard, onion and garlic. Press bacon deep into mixture. Cover pot and bake 4 hours or until beans are tender. Stir occasionally and add water if needed.

3 Remove bacon, chop into pieces and stir back in.

SERVES 8

Crockpot Red Beans and Rice

1 pound dried red kidney beans

1 ham bone (with meat) or 4 smoked ham hocks

1 bay leaf

1 teaspoon red pepper or to taste

1 clove garlic, crushed

1 stalk celery, chopped

1 large white or yellow onion, chopped

2 teaspoons sugar

2 teaspoons salt

1 teaspoon cumin

5 cups cooked white rice

Chopped fresh parsley

1 Wash beans in cold water. Place in crockpot, add water to cover by 4 inches and cook on high 2 hours.

2 Add remaining ingredients, except rice and parsley, and cook 2 or 3 hours on high.

3 Serve over rice and garnish with parsley.

SERVES 4

Mexican-Style Rice
with Beans and Cheese

2 jalapeño peppers

1 tablespoon canola or other vegetable oil

2 cloves garlic, minced

⅔ cup chopped white or yellow onion

1 cup green bell pepper or a mix of red, yellow and green bell peppers

2 tablespoons chopped cilantro leaves

1½ cups chopped fresh tomatoes

Pinch salt

1 (15-ounce) can garbanzo or red beans, drained

2 cups cooked white rice

1 cup shredded Cheddar or Monterey Jack cheese, divided

1 Slice jalapeños down the middle. If you do not enjoy spicy foods, scrape out seeds, cut away white membranes and mince only the green flesh. Otherwise, mince the whole peppers.

2 Heat oil in a large saucepan and sauté jalapeños, garlic, onion and bell peppers 5 minutes or until they just begin to wilt; stir often.

3 Stir in cilantro, tomatoes and salt, reduce heat to low and cook uncovered 5 minutes. Stir in beans, cooked rice and ½ cup cheese.

4 Preheat oven to 350°. Pour into baking pan, sprinkle on remaining ½ cup cheese and bake, uncovered, 20 minutes.

SERVES 6

How to Make Boiled Rice

This recipe can be doubled or tripled. However, for more than 12 servings (6 cups water to 3 cups raw rice), I suggest that you consider making 2 batches.

INGREDIENTS

2 parts water

1 part long-grain raw rice (do not use instant or minute rice)

1 Place water in a pot and bring to a boil.

2 Add and stir in rice.

3 When water returns to a boil, stir, cover and reduce heat to very low.

4 Allow rice to cook on very low heat 20 minutes. Do not remove lid. Do not stir.

5 Remove cooked rice from stove, remove lid, fluff and serve.

SERVES 4

VARIATIONS FOR EACH 1 CUP RAW RICE:

Substitute chicken or beef broth for water.

Add 1 to 2 tablespoons butter to the boiling water before adding rice.

Add ¼ teaspoon salt to boiling water before adding rice.

Add 2 chicken or beef bouillon cubes (no butter or salt).

Add 1 tablespoon chopped parley or chives at the same time that you add the raw rice.

Add 2 tablespoons chopped pecans, walnuts or pine nuts at the same time that you add the raw rice.

CASSEROLES

My first exposure to a proper venison casserole occurred in December of 1984. The reason I remember this month is because my hunting license is still tucked behind the picture of my first mule deer. I was new to Nevada and one of my board friends invited me to tag along with him to hunt mule deer in Charleston, Nevada, with the Prunty family. This family had home-steaded their property in the early 1880's. In 1984, the family operated a working horse and cattle ranch on which they supplemented their income with an occasional guided horseback mule deer hunt.

My friend was a rather colorful character in his own right and you would have had to have met him to have appreciated him. He came from a long line of Nevada gold prospectors. He sported a long and bushy, salt-and-pepper, Yosemite Sam-style mustache and drove a vintage sand-colored four-wheel drive Subaru station wagon. I suspect the reason that he had a sand-colored vehicle was so that it would blend in with the desert land-scape while he prospected.

My friend explained to me on the drive up that Charleston was located three miles from the 111,000-acre Jarbidge Wilderness area. In the 1980's, Jarbidge was one best-kept secrets for producing quality mule deer and the terrain is remote, steep and rugged. What I did not know was that Charleston was not actually a town—it was a geographically defined point on a map that was at the end of a fifty-plus mile, unimproved dirt/mud road.

I had never hunted mule deer; I had never hunted with a guide; I had never hunted from a horse or ridden one that much. I had never hunted

Author with His First Mule Deer

in the mountains and I had never hunted in deep snow, but the price was right—$250.00 ($83.33 per day) for three days of hunting.

Being an ol' country boy that grew up hunting whitetail deer on acorn-covered bottomland and in new-growth pine plantations, I had never seen a hunting area that was so beautiful. The scenery looked as though it came from a beer commercial—low grass meadows, mountains covered with snow, wild horses roaming the passes, and aspen-covered slopes up to the tree line. There was no doubt in my mind that I had died and gone to heaven.

On the first day, we saw no deer that were in gun range. Ten years before, I had surgery on both knees to repair the damaged caused by my parachuting and canoe racing during my "irresponsible youth days" and they were giving me one heck of a problem riding that horse. I cannot say that I had a smile on my face, but I made the ride without causing any embarrassment to myself or the others.

My ol' friend had this little hemorrhoid problem that the horse riding aggravated. When we returned to the bunkhouse after dinner, he poured himself a half water glass full of Yukon Jack and swore that he needed it to numb his little bottom problem. Since I was still limping and hobbling along, he offered me a little taste to ease my pain. If you are familiar with Yukon Jack, you already know all there is to know about that powerful beverage—a little bit goes a long way.

I should have suspected something when I read the label, "The Black Sheep of Canadian Liquors. Yukon Jack is a taste born of hoary nights, when lonely men struggled to keep their fires lit and their cabins warm." At 100 proof, in a few minutes, my half glass had completely removed my knee pain and blew the top of my head right off—all at the same time.

On day two of our hunt, around 11:00 a.m., our guide told us to dismount and he eased us around a house-size boulder. There, across the canyon, was a nice male mule deer. From what I had seen in photos of mule deer, the rack wasn't trophy size, but I had come to hunt for meat and not a wall hanger anyway. Before I could say anything, my friend said, "I'm gonna take a shot. Harold, you walk around the left side of the boulder and I'll walk around the right side." I walked around to my side, waited, and kept watching the deer walk across the hill on the other side of the valley. My friend shot and missed. He shot again and missed. And then, he shot a third time and missed. In those days, my eyes were still good. The previous weekend, I had placed fairly high in the rankings of a 2,000-yard big-bore rifle match and at 150 to 200 yards, this shot was as easy as hitting the barn door with a shotgun. I said to myself, "Three shots! Friend, you have had more chances than you would have given me and I've had enough of this foolishness. Anyway, you owe me big time for 'making' me drink that Yukon Jack last night."

When we had warmed our bodies and cleaned my deer, the guide's wife had a venison casserole ready for us at dinner. Although I did not actually see her make the casserole and I did not ask her for her recipe at the time, I have tried to re-create it in Oven-Baked Ground Venison and Potato Casserole (page 252).

After my second painful day in the saddle and the harvesting of my first mule deer, I opted to stay in camp on the third day and limp around helping with farm chores because I did not think my body could stand another day in the saddle or another dose of "pain medicine."

Baked Venison and Mustard Casserole

2 pounds venison loin, cut in 1-inch cubes

2 tablespoons all-purpose flour

2 tablespoons vegetable cooking oil

8 ounces fresh mushrooms, sliced

1 cup canned beef broth

3 tablespoons mustard

Salt and pepper to taste

Tied bundle of miscellaneous fresh herbs

1 Preheat oven to 325°. Dredge cubed venison in flour. Brown in oil and transfer to a casserole dish.

2 Sauté mushrooms in same skillet until lightly wilted and add to casserole dish, scraping pan to include drippings.

3 Combine beef broth and mustard. Add to casserole and sprinkle with salt and pepper.

4 Place tied herbs on top. Cover and cook 2 hours, stirring once during cooking.

5 Remove herbs before serving.

SERVES 4 TO 6

Creamed Cubed-Steak Casserole

INGREDIENTS

2 pounds venison steak, cubed

11 tablespoons margarine, divided

4 cups Creamed Venison Sauce

2 teaspoons celery salt

½ teaspoon pepper

6 tablespoons chopped parsley

4 teaspoons Worcestershire sauce

½ cup pickle relish

1 cup dry unseasoned breadcrumbs

CREAMED VENISON SAUCE:

3 tablespoons all-purpose flour

1½ cups canned beef broth

6 tablespoons cream

Salt and pepper to taste

1 Preheat oven to 350°. Brown venison in 3 tablespoons margarine.

2 Add a small amount of water and simmer in a covered skillet until tender. Add a little more water if needed.

3 When venison is tender, add Creamed Venison Sauce, celery salt, pepper, parsley, Worcestershire and pickle relish.

4 Grease a 4-quart casserole dish with 4 tablespoons margarine and add venison mixture.

5 Sprinkle top with breadcrumbs and dot with remaining 4 tablespoons margarine. Bake until breadcrumbs are browned.

CREAMED VENISON SAUCE:

6 Whisk flour into broth. Pour into a saucepan and cook, stirring, 1 minute or until sauce thickens. Scrape browned bits from bottom of pan.

7 Add cream and salt and pepper.

SERVES 4 TO 6

Oven-Baked Ground Venison and Potato Casserole

1 pound ground venison

4 cups peeled and sliced potatoes

1 tablespoon chopped onion

2 teaspoons salt, divided

Pepper

¾ cup evaporated milk

½ cup oatmeal

¼ cup ketchup

5 tablespoons chopped onion

1 Preheat oven to 350°. Brown venison in cooking oil in a skillet; drain.

2 Mix venison with potatoes, onion, 1 teaspoon salt and dash of pepper and place in a 2- to 3-quart casserole dish.

3 Mix remaining teaspoon of salt with remaining ingredients and spread over potatoes.

4 Cover and bake 30 to 45 minutes or until potatoes are tender.

SERVES 4 TO 6

Sour Cream, Steak and Vegetable Casserole

2 pounds venison steak, cut in 2-inch pieces

1 clove garlic, minced

Bacon grease

1 cup diced celery

1 cup diced carrots

½ cup minced onion

2 cups water

1 cup tart fruit juice

1 bay leaf, halved

8 peppercorns

1 teaspoon salt

¼ cup butter, softened

¼ cup all-purpose flour

1 cup sour cream

Salt and pepper to taste

1. Sauté venison and garlic in bacon grease until brown on all sides. Transfer to a 2-quart casserole.

2. Sauté celery, carrots and onion in drippings in skillet until just tender.

3. Add water, fruit juice, bay leaf, peppercorns and salt; blend well and pour mixture over venison.

4. Preheat oven to 300°. Cover dish and bake 45 minutes to 1 hour or until venison is tender.

5. Remove casserole from oven; drain off and reserve the liquid.

6. Melt butter in skillet and sift in flour. Gradually add reserved liquid, stirring constantly until thickened.

7. Add sour cream and additional salt and pepper to taste. Bring sauce just to a boil and pour over casserole.

SERVES 4 TO 6

Spicy Venison and Vegetable Casserole

1 small onion

1 teaspoon vegetable
  shortening

1 (18-ounce) jar beef gravy

3 cups cooked ground venison

½ cup diced cooked carrots

½ cup diced cooked celery

½ cup English peas

3 cups mashed potatoes

1 teaspoon red pepper flakes,
  optional

1 Preheat oven to 450°. Brown onion in shortening until just clear.

2 Add gravy, venison, carrots, celery and peas. Simmer 2 minutes and pour into a 2-quart casserole dish.

3 Spread mashed potatoes on top and sprinkle with pepper flakes. Bake 25 minutes or until potatoes are lightly browned.

SERVES 4

Miss Sheila's Venison and French Fry Casserole

1 pound ground venison

1 small onion, diced

Hot sauce to taste

1 (10.75-ounce) can Cheddar
  cheese soup

1 (10.75-ounce) can cream of
  celery soup

Frozen French fries

Pepper to taste

1 Preheat oven to 350°. Mix venison, onion and hot sauce. Press into bottom of 9x9-inch pan or glass casserole dish.

2 Mix cheese and celery soups. Do not add additional water. Spread over venison.

3 Cover with frozen French fries. Season with pepper. Bake 40 minutes or until French fries are golden.

SERVES 4

Baked Eggplant and Venison Sausage Casserole

INGREDIENTS

3 large eggplants, peeled and cubed

2 pounds venison sausage, sliced ¼ inch thick

2 tablespoons cooking oil

1 cup chopped celery

1 cup chopped white onion

3 green onion tops, chopped

1 (6.25-ounce) box stuffing mix, plus ingredients to prepare

½ teaspoon pepper

2 cups shredded Cheddar cheese

1 Preheat oven to 350°. In a skillet, cook eggplant with a small amount of water 10 minutes or until tender. Drain and set aside.

2 Cook sausage in skillet until just browned. Add celery and onion to skillet; sauté until vegetables are just tender. Drain and set aside.

3 Prepare stuffing mix according to package directions.

4 Combine stuffing, eggplant, sausage-vegetable mixture and pepper. Spoon into a greased 9x13-inch baking dish. Cover and bake 10 to 15 minutes.

5 Uncover and top with cheese. Bake until cheese begins to melt.

SERVES 8 TO 10

Casserole of Venison, Tomato, Lemon and Mushrooms

INGREDIENTS

4 tablespoons olive oil

1 (3-pound) venison roast, cut into 2-inch cubes

2 tablespoons all-purpose flour

1 teaspoon dried thyme

1 teaspoon salt

Pepper to taste

5 tablespoons real butter, divided

1 cup finely chopped onion

1 tablespoon minced garlic

½ cup dry white wine

1½ cups canned beef broth

1 cup seeded and coarsely chopped tomatoes

2 strips fresh lemon peel, cut 2 inches long

¾ pound fresh small whole mushrooms

2 tablespoons minced parsley

SERVES 4 TO 6

1. Preheat oven to 450°. Heat oil in a large skillet. Add meat 4 to 6 pieces at a time and sauté until browned on all sides.

2. Combine flour, thyme, salt and pepper. Dredge meat in mixture. Place meat in uncovered casserole dish and bake 10 minutes or until meat is slightly crusted. Remove from oven.

3. Reduce oven to 325°. Melt 2 tablespoons butter in skillet and sauté onion and garlic 10 minutes until browned.

4. Add wine and broth and boil a few minutes over medium heat. Scrape up bits and pour into casserole dish.

5. Stir in tomatoes and lemon peel. Bake 1 to 1½ hours or until venison is tender.

6. Melt remaining 3 tablespoons butter in skillet and sauté mushrooms; pour into casserole dish and bake 15 minutes.

7. Strain entire contents, reserving liquid. Discard lemon peel.

8. Skim fat from reserved liquid and reduce it to about 2 cups. Pour over venison.

9. Place venison and mushrooms on a large serving platter and garnish with chopped parsley.

Breakfast Casserole
with Dinner Roll Topping

1 pound venison sausage

1 (8-ounce) can refrigerated crescent dinner rolls

2 cups shredded Cheddar cheese

1 small onion, chopped

4 eggs, lightly beaten

¾ cup whole milk

¼ teaspoon salt

¼ teaspoon pepper

1 Preheat oven to 400°. Brown sausage in large skillet and drain excess fat.

2 Press crescent rolls into bottom and up sides of greased 9x13-inch glass baking dish, pinching to seal.

3 Layer with sausage, cheese and onion.

4 Combine eggs, milk and seasonings; pour over casserole. Bake 20 minutes or until eggs are set.

5 Remove from oven and let stand 5 minutes before serving.

SERVES 4

Stove-Top Venison, Mushroom and Rice Casserole

2 pounds ground venison

Salt and pepper to taste

2 cups minced celery

2 cups minced onions

1 green bell pepper, chopped

1 (10.75-ounce) can cream of mushroom soup

1 (10.5-ounce) can chicken and rice soup

1 cup uncooked long-grain white rice

1 Heat a large skillet; add oil and quickly brown venison to rare.

2 Add salt, pepper, celery, onions and green bell pepper; heat thoroughly.

3 Mix remaining ingredients and pour over venison mixture.

4 Cover and simmer over low heat 1 hour.

SERVES 8

Mushroom Venison Casserole

INGREDIENTS

4 pounds venison hindquarter steak, cubed

1 cup red wine

2 (10.75-ounce) cans cream of celery soup

1 (10.75-ounce) can cream of mushroom soup

1 (1-ounce) envelope onion soup mix

4 cups sliced fresh mushrooms

½ cup dried onions

Cooked noodles for 4

1 Place venison and wine in zip-close plastic bag and refrigerate 1 hour.

2 Preheat oven to 275°. Remove venison from marinade, discarding marinade.

3 Combine venison with soups, soup mix and mushrooms in a casserole dish.

4 Cover with dried onions. Bake 4 hours.

5 Serve over cooked noodles.

SERVES 4

Cream of Mushroom and Venison Casserole

INGREDIENTS

¼ cup red wine vinegar

1½ cups water

¼ teaspoon salt, plus more for rubbing

1½ teaspoons Worcestershire sauce, divided

4 to 5 pounds venison round steak

2 medium onions, chopped

1 garlic clove, minced

3½ tablespoons olive oil

Red pepper flakes, optional

2 (10.75-ounce) cans cream of mushroom soup

2 cups dry red wine

2 bay leaves

1 Combine vinegar, water, salt and ½ teaspoon Worcestershire sauce. Pour over venison, cover and refrigerate 8 hours or overnight.

2 Sauté onions and garlic in olive oil until onions are just clear.

3 Preheat oven to 325°. Remove venison from marinade, and rub venison with additional salt, red pepper flakes and remaining 1 teaspoon Worcestershire.

4 Place venison into ovenproof dish and add cream of mushroom soup. Cover and cook 30 minutes.

5 Add wine and bay leaves. Cook 2 more hours, basting every 20 to 30 minutes.

6 When 10 minutes of cooking time is remaining, remove cover and allow to brown. Remove bay leaves before serving.

SERVES 4 TO 6

SWEETS

Being over age 40, I rarely ever eat a dessert at home any more. However, since we are normally at deer camp for only a short period of time each year, why not enjoy and savor every moment? I am not suggesting that we eat a dessert every day, but it sure is nice when someone in the bunch feels the tug of their sweet tooth and surprises the rest of us with an after-dinner dessert.

One of the members at a hunting camp that I once belonged to had a long and established tradition of "making" a dessert for the first evening dinner of deer season. He had been doing this for longer than I had been a member and my hunting seasons were never complete without a taste of his Banana Pudding with Banana and Cinnamon Sauce (page 270). Since the pudding recipe takes more than 30 minutes to prepare, he "made" it at home and brought it along with him. But, he made the Banana and Cinnamon Sauce at camp. Knowing him as I did, I often wondered if his wife actually made the banana pudding and he was just the delivery boy. This had been such a long-standing tradition and it tasted so good, that for fear he would discontinue the tradition, I was always afraid to ask him if his wife actually made it. Some questions at deer camp, you just do not need to ask.

Although many of these desserts take less than 30 minutes to prepare, others take a little longer. The nice thing about desserts is that they can normally be made the day before and are also just as good the day after.

Sweet Green Tomato and Lemon Pie

INGREDIENTS

6 green tomatoes

5 tablespoons water, divided

½ lemon, sliced

2 tablespoons all-purpose flour

1 cup sugar

Salt to taste

Ground cinnamon to taste

2 tablespoons butter, softened

2 (8-ounce) frozen pastry pie
  crusts, thawed

Sugar for topping

1 Preheat oven to 350°. Cut green tomatoes into thin slices and cook with 2 tablespoons water and lemon slices until almost tender. Remove tomatoes, discard lemon, strain and save cooking liquid.

2 Mix flour with remaining 3 tablespoons water. When tomato liquid has cooled, mix in flour-water slurry, sugar and salt. Simmer until thickened.

3 Add tomatoes, cinnamon and butter. Pour hot tomato mixture into 1 pie crust.

4 Lay second crust on top and crimp around the edge. Sprinkle top with sugar. Bake 30 minutes or until brown.

SERVES 6

Southern Muscadine Pie

4 cups ripe muscadines

½ cup white sugar

1 (8-ounce) prepared pie crust

2 cups crushed Ritz Crackers

1 cup packed light brown sugar

¼ pound margarine or butter, melted

1 With your fingers, squeeze pulp out of each muscadine 1 at a time. Keep skins and pulp separate.

2 Cook pulp over low heat until seeds loosen. Press through a strainer or food mill to separate out seeds.

3 Preheat oven to 325°. Mix together pulp, skins and white sugar. Cook 10 to 15 minutes until skins are almost tender. Place into pie shell, cover with crackers, brown sugar and margarine. Bake 1 hour.

SERVES 6

Mississippi Buttermilk Pie

INGREDIENTS

1 (8-ounce) frozen pastry pie crust, thawed

½ cup butter, softened

1½ cups sugar

2 tablespoons all-purpose flour

1 teaspoon baking soda

3 large eggs

½ cup buttermilk

2 tablespoons vanilla extract

1 Preheat oven to 325°. Line a pie pan with pie crust.

2 Melt butter and add sugar, flour and baking soda; beat well.

3 Beat in eggs 1 at a time. Beat in buttermilk and vanilla extract. Pour into pie crust and bake 45 minutes.

SERVES 6

Miss Patsy's Blackberry and Sour Cream Pie

1 cup sugar, divided

1 cup sour cream

3 tablespoons all-purpose flour

¼ teaspoon salt

2 (8-inch) frozen pie shell crusts, thawed

4 cups fresh blackberries, raspberries or blueberries, divided

¼ cup fine unseasoned breadcrumbs

1 tablespoon butter, melted

1 Preheat oven to 375°. Combine ½ cup sugar, sour cream, flour and salt.

2 Line a pie pan with 1 pie shell. Spread half the berries on top. Lay on another pie shell and spread with remaining berries. Spread sour cream mixture on top.

3 Combine breadcrumbs, remaining sugar and melted butter. Sprinkle sweetened breadcrumbs on top.

4 Bake 40 to 45 minutes or until golden brown.

SERVES 6

Miss Anne's Blackberry Cobbler

INGREDIENTS

4 cups blackberries, blueberries or quartered strawberries

¾ cup sugar

3 tablespoons all-purpose flour

½ teaspoon cinnamon

⅛ teaspoon salt

2 (9-inch) Pillsbury pie crusts

1 teaspoon lemon juice

1 tablespoon cold butter, chopped

¼ teaspoon sugar, optional

1 Mix together fruit, sugar, flour, cinnamon and salt. Line a 9½x9½x 2-inch ovenproof baking dish with 1 pie crust.

2 Pour in filling. Pour over with lemon juice and dot with butter. Cut slits in second pie crust and press down on top of cobbler. Sprinkle with sugar and bake at 400° for 35 to 40 minutes.

TO FREEZE:

3 Before laying in first pie crust, line baking dish with heavy-duty aluminum foil and wrap over edges and down sides. Make cobbler and bake per directions. Allow to cool and place dish in freezer until frozen. Remove from freezer and lift cobbler out by aluminum foil. Fold foil over top, wrap in another layer of foil and place in freezer.

TO SERVE:

4 Remove foil, place cobbler into same size baking dish and allow to thaw. Can be served either cold or warm.

SERVES 6

Lemon Zest Pound Cake

This recipe calls for a Bundt cake pan and few deer camps have a Bundt cake pan in the pot drawer. However, these pans are very inexpensive and can be purchased at any chain discount store.

INGREDIENTS

3 cups sugar

1 cup vegetable shortening

1 cup buttermilk

2 teaspoons butter flavoring

2 teaspoons lemon flavoring

6 eggs, lightly beaten

3 cups all-purpose flour

¼ teaspoon baking soda

¼ teaspoon baking powder

½ teaspoon salt

Powdered sugar

Zest of 1 lemon

1 Preheat oven to 325°. Cut sugar into shortening.

2 Mix together buttermilk, flavorings and eggs; mix into shortening mixture.

3 Sift together flour, baking soda, baking powder and salt and slowly stir into shortening-buttermilk mixture.

4 Spray Bundt pan with nonstick spray. Pour batter into pan and bake 1¼ to 2 hours or until done. Allow to cool.

5 Invert cake pan onto a large serving plate and bump several times. Cake should drop down onto plate. Sprinkle with powdered sugar and lemon zest.

SERVES 8 TO 10

SWEETS

Scottish Cream Crowdie

2 heaping tablespoons oats

1 cup whipping cream

½ teaspoon rum or vanilla flavoring

1 cup raspberries, blueberries or blackberries

1 Toast oats in a skillet until just brown.

2 Whip the cream until frothy but not stiff. Stir in toasted oats and remaining ingredients. Chill 2 hours and serve.

3 Melted vanilla ice cream can be substituted for cream.

SERVES 4 TO 6

Baked Strawberry Custard

INGREDIENTS

⅔ cup condensed milk

2 cups hot water

3 eggs, lightly beaten

½ teaspoon salt

1 teaspoon strawberry extract

2 drops red food coloring

Strawberries and chocolate mint leaves for garnish, optional

1 Preheat oven to 325°. Mix together condensed milk and hot water. Pour milk mixture gradually over beaten eggs, stirring constantly.

2 Add salt, strawberry extract and red food coloring. Pour custard mixture into a greased baking dish or greased custard cups.

3 Place dish or cups in a pan filled with 1 inch of hot water and bake 1 hour or until custard is set.

4 Garnish and serve. Custard can also be refrigerated and served cold.

SERVES 4 TO 6

Banana Pudding

with Banana Cinnamon Sauce

This recipe calls for a double boiler and few deer camps have a double boiler in the pot drawer. However, these pots are very inexpensive and can be purchased at any chain discount store.

½ cup sugar

⅓ cup all-purpose flour

⅛ teaspoon salt

4 egg yolks, lightly beaten

2 cups whole milk

½ teaspoon vanilla extract

1 (12-ounce) box vanilla wafers

5 bananas

BANANA CINNAMON SAUCE:

1 large banana, mashed

2 tablespoons light brown sugar

¼ teaspoon ground cinnamon

1½ tablespoons margarine or butter

2 tablespoons light rum, optional

1 Sift sugar, flour and salt into top of a double boiler over boiling water.

2 Stir in egg yolks and milk and blend well. Cook, uncovered, stirring constantly until sauce thickens. Reduce heat and cook 5 minutes, stirring constantly.

3 Stir in vanilla extract and remove from heat.

4 Line a large bowl with vanilla wafers. Alternate layers of custard, banana slices and wafers. Make wafers the last layer.

5 Pour Banana and Cinnamon Sauce over top. Refrigerate at least 6 hours before serving.

BANANA CINNAMON SAUCE:

6 Place ingredients in a small saucepan and mix well. Simmer over low heat a few minutes until banana is cooked.

SERVES 6 TO 8

Old-Style Banana Pudding

This recipe, from Mrs. Clyde Elizabeth Lynch, takes a little time to make, but it is worth it. When I was a young boy, my grandmother would make two batches of this banana pudding recipe, one for the family and one just for me.

INGREDIENTS

PUDDING:

1 cup sugar

½ cup all-purpose flour

3 cups whole milk

4 egg yolks, beaten

1 tablespoon vanilla extract

3 tablespoons butter, softened

1½ cups whipping cream

MERINGUE TOPPING:

4 egg whites

¼ teaspoon cream of tartar

1 teaspoon vanilla extract

⅓ cup sugar

TO FINISH:

1 (12-ounce) box vanilla wafers

7 bananas, sliced across ¼-inch thick

SERVES 6 TO 8

1 Whisk sugar, flour and milk in heavy saucepan until smooth. Cook over medium heat, stirring constantly, just until mixture comes to a boil.

2 Remove from heat and whisk a little hot pudding into yolks. Pour yolk mixture back into pudding and whisk well. Cook 1 to 2 minutes, stirring until thick.

3 Strain; stir in vanilla and butter. Press plastic wrap directly onto surface. Chill.

4 Whip cream until stiff peaks form, fold into chilled pudding and set aside.

MERINGUE TOPPING:

5 Beat egg whites, cream of tartar and vanilla until stiff peaks form. Slowly add sugar and beat until stiff and glossy.

TO FINISH:

6 Preheat oven to 350°. In a baking dish Layer wafers, ⅓ of pudding, then ½ the bananas. Repeat layers and top with last ⅓ of pudding. Spread with meringue and bake until light golden brown, about 15 minutes. Cool to room temperature or chill in refrigerator before serving.

Rice Pudding
with Raisins and Nuts

This dish can be served hot or refrigerated and served cold.

INGREDIENTS

1 cup instant or Minute rice

1⅓ cups water

2 large eggs

2 cups milk

½ cup raisins

½ cup sugar

¼ teaspoon salt

¼ teaspoon unsweetened cocoa powder

¼ teaspoon nutmeg

¼ cup pecan or walnut bits or chopped pecans or walnuts

¼ cup almond bits or chopped almonds

1. Preheat oven to 425°. Add rice to water, stir several times and bring to a boil. Lower heat to very low, cover and simmer about 12 minutes. Rice should absorb all the water.

2. Beat eggs and pour into a ceramic or glass baking dish. Mix in cooked rice, milk, raisins, sugar, salt and cocoa powder. Sprinkle with nutmeg.

3. Bake 50 to 60 minutes, stirring occasionally. Before serving, sprinkle top or individual servings with nuts.

SERVES 6

Chocolate Pudding

2 cups whole milk, divided

3 tablespoons cornstarch

4 tablespoons sugar

¼ teaspoon salt

2 tablespoons unsweetened
  cocoa powder

1 teaspoon vanilla extract

Sweetened whipped cream

1 Scald 1½ cups milk in a heavy saucepan and set aside.

2 Whisk together cornstarch, sugar, salt and cocoa. Add remaining ½ cup milk and stir until well blended.

3 Stir in the scalded milk and blend well. Pour mixture back into the saucepan and stir constantly over medium heat until thickened. Let pudding boil 1 minute while stirring briskly.

4 Remove from heat, pour into a bowl and, when cooled, stir in vanilla extract.

5 You can eat the pudding warm, over ice cream or pour into individual serving cups. Cover and refrigerate until ready to serve. Top with sweetened whipped cream.

SERVES 4

Easy Eggnog Ice Cream

This is the easiest and quickest way to make ice cream that I have ever found. Canned Borden's eggnog is ready to use—just as is.

2 (32-ounce) cans Borden's eggnog or other prepared eggnog drink

Ice-cream machine

Ice cubes or crushed ice

Ice cream salt (in a pinch, table salt can be substituted)

Nutmeg

Mint sprigs for garnish, optional

1 Open the can of eggnog and follow directions on your machine for making ice cream.

2 When ready, sprinkle with nutmeg and garnish with a mint leaf.

Old Praline Recipe

You may wish to pour onto wax paper, rather than onto a greased cookie sheet.

INGREDIENTS

4 cups packed brown sugar

½ cup whole milk or cream

2 tablespoons real butter, softened

1 teaspoon cherry flavoring

1 pound almonds, whole and pieces

1 In a saucepan, mix together all ingredients except almonds and stir over medium heat until sugar dissolves. Bring mixture quickly to boiling point and hold at that temperature 3 minutes without stirring.

2 Remove from heat and stir in almonds. Pour in 2- to 3-inch puddles on a well-greased cookie sheet and allow to cool.

INDEX

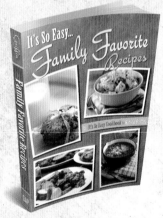

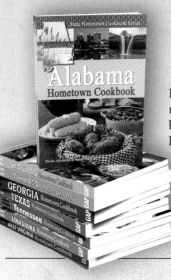

State Hometown Cookbook Series
A Hometown Taste of America, One State at a Time

Each state's hometown charm is revealed through local recipes from real hometown cooks along with stories and photos that will take you back to your hometown . . . or take you on a journey to explore other hometowns across the country.

EACH: $18.95 • 240 to 272 pages • paperbound • full-color

**Alabama • Georgia • Louisiana • Mississippi
South Carolina • Tennessee • Texas • West Virginia**

Eat & Explore Cookbook Series
Discover community celebrations and unique destinations, as they share their favorite recipes.

Experience our United States like never before when you explore the distinct flavor of each state by savoring 250 favorite recipes from the state's best cooks. In addition, the state's favorite events and destinations are profiled throughout the book with fun stories and everything you need to know to plan your family's next road trip.

EACH: $18.95 • 240 to 272 pages • 7x9 • paperbound • full-color

**Arkansas • Minnesota • North Carolina
Ohio • Oklahoma • Virginia • Washington**

State Back Road Restaurants Series
Every road leads to delicious food.

From two-lane highways and interstates, to dirt roads and quaint downtowns, every road leads to delicious food when traveling across our United States. The STATE BACK ROAD RESTAURANTS COOKBOOK SERIES serves up a well-researched and charming guide to each state's best back road restaurants. No time to travel? No problem. Each restaurant shares with you their favorite recipes—sometimes their signature dish, sometimes a family favorite, but always delicious.

EACH: $18.95 • 256 pages • 7x9 • paperbound • full-color

Alabama • Kentucky • Missouri • Tennessee • Texas

www.GreatAmericanPublishers.com • www.facebook.com/GreatAmericanPublishers

Great Gifts for Hunters and Sportsmen

Game for All Seasons

Harold Webster delights sportsmen and those who cook game with 300 seasonal recipes for venison, fish, fowl, and other delicacies from field and water. In addition to the recipes, Webster tells fascinating stories about the capturing, cleaning and cooking of the game making the book an entertaining read as well as an essential resource for creating memorable meals from any hunter's bounty.

240 pages • 7x10 • paperbound • $16.95

The Ultimate Venison Cookbook for Deer Camp

Harold Webster once again delights sportsmen with a cookbook that should be on every deer camp shelf. Not only can it be used at Deer Camp, but it also serves as your guide for cooking various venison cuts at home. With just a few ingredients and simple techniques, you can be cooking like a pro.

288 pages • 7x10 • paperbound
Full color photographs • $21.95

www.GreatAmericanPublishers.com • www.facebook.com/GreatAmericanPublishers

ORDER FORM

Mail to: Great American Publishers • 501 Avalon Way, Suite B • Brandon, MS 39047
Or call us toll-free 1.888.854.5954 to order by check or credit card.

❑ Check Enclosed

Charge to: ❑ Visa ❑ MC ❑ AmEx ❑ Disc

Card#_____

Exp Date _____

Signature_____

Name_____

Address _____

City _____ State _____ Zip _____

Phone_____

Email_____

QTY. TITLE   TOTAL

Subtotal _____

Postage ($4 first book; $1 each additional) _____
Order 5 or more books, get FREE shipping

Total _____